The God of
the Way
Study Series
· · ·

The
GOD
of
HIS
WORD

BIBLE STUDY GUIDE | SIX SESSIONS

Kathie Lee Gifford
with Rabbi Jason Sobel

HarperChristian
Resources

Contents

A Note from Kathie Lee

My passion for understanding the Scriptures is rooted in my desire to know what the Hebrew in the Old Testament and the Greek in the New Testament actually *say*. King David wrote, "As for God, his way is perfect: the LORD's *word is flawless*" (Psalm 18:30, emphasis added). So, it's important for us to know the original words the authors used when they wrote God's Word.

As I've grown in my knowledge and understanding of the Scriptures through decades of study and rabbinical trips to the Holy Land to deepen my experience, I've grown ever more passionate to pass along what many of my teachers, who have vastly more knowledge and insight than I do, have shared with me about the Word of God. For example, consider that there are more than one hundred names for God mentioned in the Bible. Imagine that!

I love that there are specific names, though, for various aspects of God's nature—many of which we will cover in this study. *El Roi*, for the God Who Sees. *Jehovah Jireh*, for the God Who Provides. *Jehovah Elohim*—one of my favorites—for the God who Creates.

And he's not just the creator of everything that has come before. He is the God of all creation and is creating new things *even this moment*. In Isaiah 43:19, the Lord says, "See, I am doing a new thing! Now it springs up; do you not perceive it? I am making a way in the wilderness and streams in the wasteland." In other words, God is saying, "Hey, look around, everybody! I am the God who never changes! I am doing brand-new miracles all over the cosmos—and even in your life! Open your eyes! Open your hearts!"

I also find it interesting that when God was creating the first humans to populate the earth, he spoke these words: "Let *us* make mankind in *our* image, in *our* likeness, so that they may rule over the fish in the sea and the birds in the sky, over the livestock and all the wild animals, and over all the creatures that move along the ground" (emphasis added).

Who is this *us* and *our* that this verse in Genesis refers to? The New Testament's complementary passage, John 1:1, tells us, "In the beginning was the Word, and the Word was with God, and the Word was God." This is profound in every way. John is stating that Jesus was not only *with* God at the beginning of creation but also *was* God—that he created all things. Jehovah God (Adonai), Jesus (his only begotten Son), and the Holy Spirit (the

Ruach, or "breath" of God) worked together to bring all things to pass—and still work together to sustain all things.

But we learn even more eye-popping revelations just a few verses later in John's Gospel: "The Word became flesh and made his dwelling among us" (verse 14). The same Word who spoke all of creation into existence is the same Word who followed the will of his Father to come to earth in human form and be born to a virginal teenage peasant girl in order to provide the ultimate sacrifice of His blood for the salvation of all of humankind.

Who among us can even begin to fathom the depth of the mystery of such a cosmic event? Only the creator himself. But the Bible tells us in John 14:7–9 that Jesus is the reflection of the face of the Father. When we see Jesus, we literally see God incarnate.

Jesus walked the earth he created so he could teach us how to walk in this world as he did. He promised that if we believe in him and the One who sent him, we, too, could do all things in his name. We, too, could learn how to truly love and truly forgive. We, too, could have the strength to carry our cross and sacrifice our will for the Father's. And ultimately, because of Jesus' death, we, too, could be resurrected into eternal life with our Creator.

I am stunned by God's grace and overwhelmed by his incomprehensible love for me, because I know I don't deserve it. We read in Isaiah 64:6, "All of us have become like one who is unclean, and all our righteous acts are like filthy rags." The Hebrew word for "filthy rags" refers to menstrual rags. Being a woman, I am completely familiar with what that means.

But the Bible also tells us in Isaiah 1:18 that Jesus has forgiven us of all unrighteousness and made us as white as snow—completely new creatures. We don't worship a God we have to visit in a building once a week. No, in him we "live and move and have our being" (Acts 17:28). Every second of every hour of every day of our existence, he is the giver of "every good and perfect gift" and the lover of our soul (James 1:17).

God put Adam and Eve in the Garden of Eden to work after his work was finished and to have dominion over everything that he had entrusted to them. This truth has *never changed*. We were also created to cocreate with *Jehovah Elohim*! Our work should still reflect our relationship with the living God we worship—the Holy (*Kadosh*) God but also Abba Father, the loving and compassionate God who longs to protect and guide his children into all blessing.

How to Use This Guide

The Scriptures reveal that the God we serve is not some impersonal being who just created the earth (and everything we know) and then stepped back to let it run its course. No, the God we serve is a *personal* being who desires to have an *intimate* relationship with us. As Jesus said, "Here I am! I stand at the door and knock. If anyone hears my voice and opens the door, I will come in and eat with that person, and they with me" (Revelation 3:20).

In this study, we will explore several important characteristics of God as revealed in the pages of his Word. We will start with the *creative* aspects of God through his design of the world and humankind. We will examine aspects of his *mercy* and his *power*. We will also look at the ways in which God provides *wisdom* to us today and reveals the way that we should go by casting his divine *light* on our path. Finally, we will examine the inclusive aspects of God's nature and discover that he is truly a God who invites *all people* to come to him.

Before you begin, keep in mind there are a few ways you can go through this material. You can experience this study with others in a group (such as a Bible study, Sunday school class, or any other small-group gathering), or you may choose to go through the content on your own. Either way, know that the videos for each session are available for you to view at any time by following the instructions provided on the inside cover of this study guide.

Group Study

Each of the sessions are divided into two parts: (1) a group study section, and (2) a personal study section. The group study section is intended to provide a basic framework on how to open your time together, get the most out of the video content, and discuss the key ideas together that were presented in the teaching. Each session includes the following:

- **Welcome:** A short note about the topic of the session for you to read on your own before you meet together as a group.

- **Connect:** A few icebreaker questions to get you and your group members thinking about the topic and interacting with each other.
- **Watch:** An outline of the key points that will be covered in each video teaching to help you follow along, stay engaged, and take notes.
- **Discuss:** Questions to help your group reflect on the material presented and apply it to your lives. In each session, you will be given four "suggested" questions and four "additional" questions to use as time allows.
- **Respond:** A short personal exercise to help reinforce the key ideas.
- **Pray:** A place for you to record prayer requests and praises for the week.

If you are doing this study in a group, make sure you have your own copy of this study guide so you can write down your thoughts, responses, and reflections and have access to the videos via streaming. You will also want to have a copy of the *God of the Way* book, as reading it alongside the curriculum will provide you with deeper insights. (See the notes at the beginning of each group session and personal study section on which chapters of the book you should read before the next group session.) Finally, keep these points in mind:

- **Facilitation:** If you are doing this study in a group, you will want to appoint someone to serve as a facilitator. This person will be responsible for starting the video and keeping track of time during discussions and activities. If *you* have been chosen for this role, there are some resources in the back of this guide that can help you lead your group through the study.

- **Faithfulness:** Your small group is a place where tremendous growth can happen as you reflect on the Bible, ask questions, and learn what God is doing in other people's lives. For this reason, be fully committed and attend each session so you can build trust and rapport with the other members.

- **Friendship:** The goal of any small group is to serve as a place where people can share, learn about God, and build friendships. So seek to make your group a "safe place." Be honest about your thoughts and feelings . . . but also listen carefully to everyone else's thoughts, feelings, and opinions. Keep anything personal that your group members share in confidence so that you can create a community where people can heal, be challenged, and grow spiritually.

If you are going through this study on your own, read the opening Welcome section and reflect on the questions in the Connect section. Watch the video and use the prompts provided to take notes. Finally, personalize the questions and exercises in the Discuss and Respond sections. Close by recording any requests you want to pray about during the week.

Personal Study

As the name implies, the personal study is for you to go work through on your own during the week. Each exercise is designed to help you explore the key ideas you uncovered during your group time and delve into passages of Scripture that will help you apply those principles to your life. Go at your own pace, doing a little each day or all at once, and spend a few moments in silence to listen to what God might be saying to you. Each personal study will include:

- **Opening:** A brief introduction to lead you into the personal study for the day.
- **Scripture:** A few passages on the topic of the day for you to read and review.
- **Reflection:** Questions for you to answer related to the passages you just read.
- **Prayer:** A prompt to help you express what you've studied in a prayer to God.

If you are doing this study as part of a group, and you are unable to finish (or even start) these personal studies for the week, you should still attend the group time. Be assured that you are still wanted and welcome even if you don't have your "homework" done. The group studies and personal studies are intended to help you hear what God wants you to hear and how to apply what he is saying to your life. So . . . as you go through this study, be listening for him to speak to you as you learn about what it means to trust in the *God of His Word*.

WEEK 1

BEFORE GROUP MEETING	Read pages 81–87 in chapter 6 of *The God of the Way* Read the Welcome section (page 3)
GROUP MEETING	Discuss the Connect questions Watch the video teaching for session 1 Discuss the questions that follow as a group Do the closing exercise and pray (pages 3–12)
PERSONAL STUDY – DAY 1	Complete the daily study (pages 14–15)
PERSONAL STUDY – DAY 2	Complete the daily study (pages 16–17)
PERSONAL STUDY – DAY 3	Complete the daily study (pages 18–19)
PERSONAL STUDY – DAY 4	Complete the daily study (pages 20–21)
PERSONAL STUDY – DAY 5 (before week 2 group meeting)	Complete the daily study (pages 22–23) Read pages 87–96 in chapter 6 in *The God of the Way* Complete any unfinished personal studies

God of Creation

אלהים

ELOHIM
[ALL MIGHTY GOD]

The heavens declare the glory of God;
the skies proclaim the work of his hands.

PSALM 19:1

Welcome | Read On Your Own

In works of fiction, there are *flat characters* and *round characters*. Flat characters are the ones you don't get to know very well. They make a few appearances, but you don't get a lot of information about them. Round characters, on the other hand, are integral to the story. By the end, you know exactly where they came from and why they do what they do. You can even anticipate their next moves based on how well you have gotten to know them.

God is a "round character." He doesn't just appear at the start of the story and then fade into the background. No, he is present on every page of Scripture—speaking with his people, encouraging them, instructing them . . . and, yes, disciplining them at times when they get off course. Truly, "the eyes of the LORD are everywhere" (Proverbs 15:3).

What's more, God has revealed his character to us through his Word. He is a *creator* and *judge*. He is *merciful* and *powerful*. He is *wise* and full of *light*. He invites *all* to follow him. He is not distant and impersonal. Rather, the Bible informs us that God is so involved in our lives that he chose to send his only Son into this world to become one of us (see John 1:1, 14).

Over the course of the next few weeks, you and your group will study these character traits and attributes of God. In this first session, you will look at the first name used for God in the Bible—*Elohim*—and what it says about him as the all-powerful creator and judge of the universe. You will discover, as so many others have discovered before you, that God has the ability to create something good out of what was once chaos and bring wholeness to this broken world.

Connect | 15 minutes

If you or any of your group members don't know each other, take a few minutes to introduce yourselves. Then, to get things started, discuss one of the following questions:

- How would you describe your primary goal or hope for participating in this study? (In other words, why are you here?)

— or —

- Do you know the significance of your name—either its meaning or why your parents gave it to you? If so, share with the group.

Watch | 20 minutes

Now it's time to watch the video for this session, which you can access by playing the DVD or through streaming (see the instructions provided on the inside front cover). As you watch, use the following outline to record any thoughts or concepts that stand out to you.

I. Why are names so significant in the Bible?

    A. Names are important in Scripture because they give us insight and revelation.

        1. The word for *soul* in Hebrew is *neshama*. The middle letters of that word are *shin* and *mem,* which forms the word *name*. At the center of the Hebrew word for *soul* is *name*.

        2. A person's name in Scripture is meant to reveal the essence of their soul. People were named or renamed to reveal something significant about their identity, calling, and mission.

    B. The names of God in Scripture likewise reveal attributes of his nature.

        1. The first name given for God is Elohim (see Genesis 1:1). This name declares God as the all-powerful creator and point to him as the supreme judge and ruler of the universe.

        2. Elohim is associated with God's attribute of strict justice (*middat hadin*). God initially created the world measure for measure. But he knew the world could not endure strict justice.

A Rabbi Like No Other

When we look at the life and teachings of Jesus, we have to remember that the people of his day would have considered him a *rabbi*—one who was learned in the Jewish Scriptures and other religious literature. The primary duty of a rabbi was to teach the Torah. He would select a group of disciples and train them in all things related to knowledge of the Torah.[1]

But the Jewish people had never encountered a rabbi like Jesus! He not only brought a depth of understanding to the Scriptures but also taught with an authority the people had never experienced before. In one story told in the Gospel of John, we read that Jesus was teaching in Jerusalem, and the Jewish people were amazed at what they were hearing. They asked, "How did this man get such learning without having being taught?" Jesus replied, "My teaching is not my own. It comes from the one who sent me" (John 7:15–16).

Jesus also demonstrated the power behind his words through miracles. A story in the Gospel of Mark tells of a time when Jesus fell asleep in the stern of a boat as his disciples crossed the Sea of Galilee. When a furious storm arose, the disciples cried out in fear, "Teacher, don't you care if we drown?" Jesus got up and revealed that he was the embodiment of Elohim—the all-powerful God who has control over creation. "He got up, rebuked the wind and said to the waves, 'Quiet! Be still!' Then the wind died down and it was completely calm" (Mark 4:38–39).

Jesus calmed the winds, the waves, and the storms on that day. These are the very things that represent chaos in our world. In its place he brought *shalom* . . . his perfect peace.

3. A second name for God—the divine name that is often translated as *Jehovah*—is associated with God's attribute of mercy (*middat rachamim*). God tempers his strict justice with his mercy.

II. What does the name Elohim reveal about God as the creator and sustainer of all things?

A. Elohim is the plural form of the name of God (El). Everything that exists in the cosmos came about through the hand of Elohim.

1. Elohim and the Hebrew word for nature (*hateva*) both have a numerical value of 86. Elohim is the creator of nature, controller of nature, and he is revealed through nature.

2. People looked at the heavens and made the mistake of thinking the creation was the Creator. Ultimately, God had to give further revelation to bring people out of idolatry.

B. We still fall into the sin of idolatry today—we turn to astrology and put our faith in the stars instead of going a little higher and putting our faith in the One who made the stars.

1. The Bible reveals there is a God who has created everything—including us—and that we can get to know him on a personal and intimate level.

2. There is an order to everything and someone who is in control of everything. This should bring great comfort and encouragement to us in this life.

III. What does the name Elohim reveal about God's attribute of justice?

A. God is the merciful creator and sustainer of all things, but he is also the One who holds the world accountable. Our actions always have consequences.

1. On a spiritual level, we will reap what we sow (see Galatians 6:7). All of us are going to have to stand before God one day and give an account of our life.

2. Just as there are natural laws, there are spiritual laws. If we don't understand the spiritual laws that God has given to us, it will create chaos in our lives, in our community, and in our world.

B. Elohim controls the chaos in this world. He brings order, light, and life out of the chaos.

1. In the Bible, chaos represents evil, sin, and death. Our world is more chaotic than ever, but when we call upon Elohim, he can bring order out of the chaos.

2. Elohim is the one who can create something out of nothing. He can take the nothingness in our lives and create something good and worthwhile out of it.

IV. How can Jesus have been with Elohim at the creation of the world?

A. The first prayer that every Jewish child learns is the Shema: "Hear, O Israel: The LORD our God, the LORD is one" (Deuteronomy 6:4). The prayer states *the Lord is one.*

B. The word for *one* in Hebrew is *echad,* and it doesn't refer to a strict oneness. The word is used when God says the husband and wife are to "become one flesh" (Genesis 2:24). They are two separate individuals, but they are called to join together to become one.

C. This idea of unified multiplicity applies even to the name Elohim, which, as we have seen, is in the plural. So even in the name Elohim, there is an allusion to the Trinity.

D. There are also allusions to the Trinity when God said, "Let us make mankind in our image" (Genesis 1:26), and when David wrote, "The LORD says to my lord: 'Sit at my right hand'" (Psalm 110:1). Ultimately, the fuller revelation comes in the person of Yeshua in the New Testament.

A God of Justice

The Bible reveals that when Elohim created the first humans, he made them in his own image and likeness (see Genesis 1:26). Part of what it means to be created in the image of God is to reflect his essence and nature. This includes reflecting his attribute of *justice*.

We find references to God's justice throughout the pages of Scripture. According to Psalm 89:14, "Righteousness and justice are the foundation of [God's] throne." Moses said to the Israelite people, "[God] is the Rock, his works are perfect, and all his ways are just" (Deuteronomy 32:4). Isaiah declared, "The LORD longs to be gracious to you. . . . For the LORD is a God of justice" (Isaiah 30:18). The prophet Micah noted, "What does the LORD require of you? To act justly and to love mercy and to walk humbly with your God" (Micah 6:8).

When we come to the New Testament, we see that Jesus' heart was always turned toward those who were oppressed, discriminated against, and ostracized from society. He was never harsh with those who admitted they were sinners and in need of God's grace. Rather, the strongest rebukes we find coming from Christ were those against the religious leaders. In one notable passage, he even pronounced seven "woes" against these individuals (see Matthew 23:13–39). Jesus was so harsh toward them because they were perverting God's justice.

Justice *matters* to God and was *modeled* by Christ. As followers of God—and those who are created in his image—justice should also matter to *us*. As James concluded in his epistle, "Religion that God our Father accepts as pure and faultless is this: to look after orphans and widows in their distress and to keep oneself from being polluted by the world" (James 1:27).

Discuss | 35 minutes

Take some time to discuss what you just watched by answering the following questions. There are some suggested questions below to help you begin your discussion, but feel free to pick any of the additional questions as well as time allows.

Suggested Questions

1. The word for *soul* in Hebrew is *neshama*. It first appears in Scripture is in Genesis 2:7: "The Lord God formed man of the dust of the ground, and breathed into his nostrils the breath of life; and man became a living soul" (KJV). What is the significance of the word *neshama*? What does it tell us about the significance of names in the Bible?

2. Read Genesis 1:1–5. In this passage, God creates the heavens and the earth and separates the light from the darkness. The Hebrew name for God used in this passage is Elohim. What does this reveal about the nature and character of God?

3. Elohim is used elsewhere in Scripture. Read Exodus 20:1–17. What does Elohim mean in this context? What does this passage reveal about the nature of God?

4. The name Elohim denotes God as the all-powerful creator of the universe—the one who brought something good out of nothing. What are some areas of your life today where you need God to create something good out of what seems like a chaotic situation?

Additional Questions

5. Read Mark 4:35–41. In this passage, Jesus is sleeping in the stern of a boat while a storm rages all around him. Notice the difference between the way the disciples and Jesus reacted to the events. How did Jesus embody the nature of Elohim in this story?

6. The Bible reveals that God created the world out of a state of chaos: "The earth was formless and empty, darkness was over the surface of the deep, and the Spirit of God was hovering over the waters" (Genesis 1:2). What does chaos typically represent in Scripture? How have you experienced this type of chaos in your life?

7. Read Isaiah 26:3. The opposite of chaos is *shalom*, a Hebrew term used in this verse that refers to the peace, harmony, wholeness, and tranquility that comes from God. What promise is found in this verse? How do we obtain *shalom* in our lives?

8. The Bible contains many different names of God that point to certain aspects of his character. If you were to give God a name based on what you know of him and how you most often picture him in your mind, what would that name be?

Respond | 10 minutes

Review the outline for the video teaching and any notes you took. In the space below, write down your most significant takeaway from this session.

Pray | 10 minutes

Praying for one another is one of the most important things you can do as a community. So use this time wisely and make it more than just a "closing prayer" to end your group experience. Be intentional about sharing your prayers, reviewing how God is answering your prayers, and actually praying for each other as a group. Use the space below to write down any requests so that you and your group members can continue to pray about them in the week ahead.

Name	Request

Personal Study

Y ou are on a journey toward a better understanding of the God of His Word. A key part of that growth, regardless of where you are spiritually, involves studying Scripture. This is the goal of these personal studies—to help you explore what the Bible has to say and how to apply the Word of God to your life. As you work through each of these exercises, be sure to write down your responses to the questions, as you will be given a few minutes to share your insights at the start of the next session if you are doing this study with others. If you are reading *The God of the Way* alongside this study, first review pages 81–87 in chapter 6 of the book.

—Day 1—

Perceptions of God

When you imagine God, what comes to mind? A person in the sky looking down on you? A kind grandfather giving you all the things you want? An elusive spirit hovering over the earth? Even though we *can't* comprehend God, our minds lock onto an image of him that we *can* comprehend. Often, these images relate to the way we view him— as an authoritarian, or a celestial Santa Claus who meets our every request, or as an impersonal force in the world.

We all create such images of God in our heads. But our imaginations are limited, and thus tend to limit God. God is so much more than we can fathom!

As you discussed this week, the first name for God that appears in Scripture is Elohim: "In the beginning [Elohim] created the heavens and the earth" (Genesis 1:1). The name Elohim appears 2,750 times in the Old Testament.[2] The term is derived from the Hebrew word El, which can mean "power" or "might," and is connected to God not only as creator but also as *judge*.[3] We see this aspect of God's nature when he gives Moses the Ten Commandments: "Moses turned and went down the mountain with the two tablets of the covenant law in his hands. . . .The tablets were the work of [Elohim]" (Exodus 32:15–16).

God goes by many names in Scripture. He is Jehovah Jireh, "the God who provides." El Roi, "the God who sees." El Elyon, "the sovereign God," and the list goes on. He cannot be captured by one name, just as he cannot be captured by pictures in our imaginations. But learning about the different names of God *can* help us to let go of any misguided ideas of what he is like and open our hearts and minds to an understanding of who he really is.

Read | Psalm 131:1–3 and Psalm 91:1–4

Reflect

1. God is often pictured in Scripture as a loving heavenly Father, but the author of Psalm 131 gives us a completely different image of God. Look especially at verse 2

in this psalm. How does the author depict God? What stands out to you the most about this imagery?

2. The author of Psalm 91 sets up his depiction of God by stating the Lord will protect us "from the fowler's snare" (verse 3). What imagery does the author then use to describe God? What is he saying about God's nature based on this image?

3. When you imagine God, what pictures and descriptions come to mind? What does God look like? Where is he located? Where do you think these images come from?

4. The psalmists used imagery of a mother calming her child and a bird protecting her young to demonstrate qualities of God that stood out to them. What attribute of God stands out you the most right now? What image would best capture that attribute?

Pray | Think about the attributes of God found in Scripture and thank him for his love, protection, and care. Whatever you need from God today, remember that he is bigger, more powerful, more loving, and more compassionate than you are imagining him to be!

-Day 2-

God's Glory in Nature

Charles Spurgeon, a famous preacher who lived in the latter half of the nineteenth century, once declared, "Doth not all nature around me praise God? . . . Doth not the thunder praise Him as it rolls like drums in the march of the God of armies? Do not the mountains praise Him when the woods upon their summits wave in adoration? Doth not the lightning write His name in letters of fire? Hath not the whole earth a voice? And shall I, can I, silent be?"[4]

If you've ever visited a place like Yosemite, Redwood National Park, the Grand Canyon, or any other scenic vista that has taken your breath away with its beauty, you can understand this kind of wonder toward God. Nature is truly awe-inspiring—and its creator, Elohim, is even more so. As the prophet Jeremiah wrote, "Sovereign LORD, you have made the heavens and the earth by your great power and outstretched arm. Nothing is too hard for you" (Jeremiah 32:17).

Nature is a beautiful gift from God for us to enjoy and steward well. But it is also a reminder of his continual presence and power—and that nothing is too hard for him to accomplish. In nature, we find babbling brooks and roaring seas. Peaceful forests and wildfires. Quenching rain and raging hurricanes. God is as peaceful as he is powerful, as merciful as he is just, as capable of building up as he is tearing down. Nature speaks of its creator.

"Doth not all nature around me praise God?" If you want to know the nature of God, look no further than nature itself. And when you do, don't be silent but declare his glory.

Read | Job 12:7–10 and Psalm 19:1–4

Reflect

1. Job had endured many crises in a short amount of time. He had lost his children, his livelihood, and his health in the span of a few days (see Job 1–2). While he could have

listened to his wife's advice to "curse God and die" (2:9), he chose a different course. What do his words in Job 12:7–10 reveal about his understanding of God?

2. Job invites his listeners to "ask the animals" about what the Lord has done (verse 7). For Job, nature itself spoke of God's power and divine work in this world. When is a time in your life that you saw God demonstrate his power to you? What happened in that situation?

3. In Psalm 19:1–2, King David writes that the very skies and heavens glorify God and reveal his knowledge to his people. What does it mean that nature "declares" God's glory? What kind of "knowledge" do God's creative works in this world reveal?

4. Think about one of your favorite places to be in nature. Picture the scenery there and what you encountered the last time that you were in that place. What could this location that you love in nature teach you about the character of God?

Pray | If you are able, spend time in prayer outside. Go on a meditative walk, look at the trees, watch the clouds—anything that will allow you to spend some time in Elohim's creation. Thank God and praise him for what you see. Ask him to continue to reveal his nature to you.

— Day 3 —

God's Desire for Justice

Have you ever felt wronged? Perhaps a neighbor cut down a tree that was on your side of the property line. Or a coworker accused you of a mistake you didn't make. Or you loaned a friend some money and he or she never paid you back. While we may disagree on exactly what justice looks like, we all know what it *feels* like. We have an innate sense of right and wrong, and we can feel it when we have been wronged (or have done wrong).

This sense of justice is a manifestation of the character of God within us. The name Elohim reflects this trait. In addition to associating God as the creator, Elohim is used in Scripture where God is acting as judge. For instance, as we saw in this week's study, it is the name used for God when he gives the Ten Commandments to Moses. The Lord wanted his people to not succumb to lawlessness now that they were out from Egypt's rule.

The Bible reveals that we serve a God who *values* justice. He told the prophet Isaiah, "I, the LORD, love justice; I hate robbery and wrongdoing" (Isaiah 61:8). He said to the prophet Micah, "What does the LORD require of you? To act justly and love mercy and to walk humbly with your God" (Micah 6:8). Later, Paul would write, "Do not take revenge, my dear friends, but leave room for God's wrath, for it is written: 'It is mine to avenge; I will repay,' says the Lord" (Romans 12:19).

The name Elohim reveals God not only as the creator but also as the judge and ruler of that creation. He cares about justice in our world today. We may look around at the chaos we sense around us and wonder if he is still active. But we can always be assured, "Many are the plans in a person's heart, but it is the LORD's purpose that prevails" (Proverbs 19:21).

Read | Psalm 89:14–18

Reflect

1. While little is known about Ethan the Ezrahite, the author of this psalm, the Bible implies that he was a wise man—though less wise than King Solomon (see 1 Kings

4:31). What wisdom does Ethan relate in this passage about the foundation of God's throne (see Psalm 89:14)?

2. The psalmist goes on to state that those who walk in the light of God's presence are blessed and celebrate God's righteousness (see verses 15–16). What do you think he means when he then writes, "Our shield belongs to the LORD" (verse 18)?

3. The Hebrew term for God's attribute of strict judgment is *middat hadin.* It is connected to God judging people according to the principle of cause-and-effect or "reaping what you sow." When are times you experienced this kind of judgment for your actions?

4. God tempers his strict justice with another attribute—his divine mercy (Hebrew *middat rachamim.*) Were God to only demonstrate his justice, we would all receive what we have reaped—eternal judgment. But instead, God put his judgment for our sins on his Son: When are times you received God's mercy when you deserved judgment?

Pray | Thinking about God as a judge can surface many thoughts, images, and feelings. In your prayer time today, let yourself sit with these thoughts, even if they are uncomfortable. Ask God where they came from. Ask him to reveal what his mercy and justice really look like.

— Day 4 —
God's Desire for Order

Home renovation shows are popular for a reason: they offer the oh-so-satisfying before-and-after. When you first meet a family on these shows, they are living in a house that is out-of-date and no longer meets their needs. But then the hosts appear with a plan. In short order, a construction crew arrives to begin the demolition. Things get much worse, but then, thirty to sixty minutes later, the house is transformed into a picture-perfect model of a modern home.

While our definitions of "order" may differ, when we achieve what we consider to be orderly—whether it is cleaning out the garage or putting the dishes away—we feel a sense of satisfaction and peace. Psychologists point to many other benefits as well. People who live in an "ordered" way spend less time looking for lost things and miss fewer deadlines. Studies also show they are more charitable and make healthier choices.[5]

Jehovah Elohim brought order to chaos when he created the earth. The world was in a state of *tohu vavohu*, as the Hebrew Scriptures tell us, which translates to "chaos and empty."[6] By creating, God brought order to the chaos. He created light and darkness, sea and earth, man and woman, animals of the sea, animals of the air. A place and category for each living thing.

When we create, we do what God did: bring order to chaos. Whether we are organizing items in a messy closet or organizing complicated feelings into a poem, song, or painting, whenever we bring order to chaos, we are partaking in creative work, which is the work of God. So the next time you find yourself drawn to a before-and-after photo, remember that is the work of God in you, the creator who craves and creates order in your life.

Read | 1 Corinthians 14:26–33

Reflect

1. In this passage, we find the apostle Paul addressing a problem that had arisen in the church in Corinth. Evidently, their worship services were chaotic, with everyone

speaking out of turn, and had even become offensive to the unbelievers who visited. What does Paul say the goal must be in their worship services (see verse 26)?

2. Paul's instructions to the congregation boil down to a few basic commands: (1) keep the number of speakers in the worship service to a minimum (see verse 27); (2) speak one at a time (see verse 27); and (3) everyone else listen and weigh what is said (see verse 29). How do you think these instructions would have aided in restoring order?

3. Paul concludes with the statement that his instructions should be followed because "God is not a God of disorder but of peace" (verse 33). What do you feel is the connection between order and peace? When have you witnessed this in your life?

4. The Bible states that before God began creating the world, "the earth was formless and empty" (Genesis 1:2). God created *order* out of *chaos*. What is chaotic in your life right now and why? How do you want God to transform that chaos into order and peace?

Pray | Think about any areas of chaos or disorder in your life. Bring those areas to God and ask him to bring you peace as you lay them before him and submit them to his control.

Day 5

God's Bond with Us

We can uncover a wealth of knowledge about who God is and how he feels about us by simply studying the name *Elohim*. As previously mentioned, the name Elohim is in the plural. The singular form is *El*, which comes from a root word meaning might, strength, or power. In the Old Testament, the name El was almost always qualified by other terms when used of the one true God, which distinguished the God of the Israelites from the false gods of the day.[7]

What's interesting is that the pairing of El + another qualifying term was often used in people's names. We see this, for example, in the name **El**ijah, which means "El is Yahweh." In **El**isha, which means "El is salvation." In Samu**el**, which means "heard by El." In Isra**el**, which means "struggles with El" (see Genesis 32:28). And we even see it in angelic names, such as Gabri**el**, which means "El is my strength," and Micha**el**, which means, "Who is like El?"[8]

These names served as a reminder of the bond that God had established with his people. For the Israelites, God wasn't just a powerful force that created the world and then moved on. He was active, present, and always at work in their lives.

Elohim has always been a God who wants to draw near to his people. This was never more evident than when Jesus came to earth, taking on the name Immanu**el**, which means "God with us." God does not want to be above you, below you, or waiting for you in some far-off heaven. He wants to be here with you *now*, in your worst moments, in your deepest desperation, in your biggest fears. In all times and places, he wants you to know *he is with you*.

Read | John 1:1–14

Reflect

1. This passage is often called the "prologue" to John's Gospel and serves to sum up the entire theme of the book. What does John say was the relationship that Jesus (here called "the Word") had with God (see verses 1–3)?

2. John describes Jesus as "the true light that gives light to everyone" (verse 9). Some did not accept that light and rejected his message. However, what is the promise given for those who do choose to receive and walk in Christ's light (see verses 12–13)?

3. John writes that "the Word became flesh and made his dwelling among us" (verse 14). What does this say about the bond that God wants to continue to have with his people?

4. When is a time that God felt incredibly near to you and you really sensed that he had "made his dwelling" in your life? How near or far does he seem from you today?

Pray | Spend a few minutes reflecting on this week's personal study time. Did God convict you of anything this week? Did you change in any way? Or learn something new? Talk to God about what you learned this week and what he might be showing you today.

For Next Week

Before you meet again with your group next week, read pages 87–96 in chapter 6 of *The God of the Way*. Also go back and complete any of the study and reflection questions from this personal study that you weren't able to finish.

WEEK 2

BEFORE GROUP MEETING	Read pages 87–96 in chapter 6 of *The God of the Way* Read the Welcome section (page 27)
GROUP MEETING	Discuss the Connect questions Watch the video teaching for session 2 Discuss the questions that follow as a group Do the closing exercise and pray (pages 27–38)
PERSONAL STUDY – DAY 1	Complete the daily study (pages 40–41)
PERSONAL STUDY – DAY 2	Complete the daily study (pages 42–43)
PERSONAL STUDY – DAY 3	Complete the daily study (pages 44–45)
PERSONAL STUDY – DAY 4	Complete the daily study (pages 46–47)
PERSONAL STUDY – DAY 5 (before week 3 group meeting)	Complete the daily study (pages 48–49) Read pages 97–100 in chapter 7 in *The God of the Way* Complete any unfinished personal studies

God of Mercy

יהוה אלהים

JEHOVAH ELOHIM

[ALL MERCIFUL GOD]

*The LORD is compassionate and gracious,
slow to anger, abounding in love.*

PSALM 103:8

Welcome | Read On Your Own

In the last session you learned about Elohim, the first name given in Scripture for God, which describes him as creator and judge. You explored how God created the world according to his attribute of strict justice—which means people would be held accountable measure-for-measure according to their actions. However, God knew that if everything in the world was cause-and-effect, it would not endure. So God tempered his justice with another name.

It can be intimidating to think of God strictly as Elohim—as the almighty creator and judge of everything that exists. But the name God chose to temper his strict justice reveals that he is not too distant nor too mighty to come down to our level. This name is *Jehovah*, the holiest name in Scripture for God, and points to his attribute of *mercy*. The name appears early in the creation account: "This is the account of the heavens and the earth when they were created, when [Jehovah Elohim] made the earth and the heavens" (Genesis 2:4).

Jehovah points to God as merciful redeemer. He saved his people in Egypt from slavery (see Exodus 3:7–10). He raised up judges to deliver them after they settled in the Promised Land (see Judges 2:16). He promised to bring them back from captivity after they had been taken into exile (see Jeremiah 29:14). Ultimately, Jehovah Elohim redeemed *all* people by sending his Son into the world to pay the price for their sins: "For God so loved the world that he gave his one and only Son, that whoever believes in him shall not perish but have eternal life" (John 3:16). Jesus is the greatest example of God's mercy toward his creation.

In this session, you will learn about Jehovah Elohim, how he interacted with humankind, and how Jesus is the ultimate manifestation of his grace.

Connect | 15 minutes

Welcome to session 2 of *The God of His Word*. If you or any of your group members are not yet acquainted, take a few minutes to introduce yourselves. Then, to get things started, discuss one of the following questions:

- What is a key insight or takeaway from last week's personal study that you would like to share with the group?

— *or* —

- Over the past week, how have you experienced God's mercy?

Watch | 20 minutes

Now watch the video for this session (remember that you can access this video via streaming by following the instructions printed on the inside front cover). As you watch, use the following outline to record any thoughts or concepts that stand out to you.

I. What does the name *Jehovah* reveal about God?

A. The name *Jehovah* is associated with God's attribute of mercy, *middat rachamim*.

1. *Rachamim* means mercy, but the root comes from the word for *womb*. When a mother has a baby in her womb and the child is born, she is moved to compassion for that child.

2. "As a father has compassion on his children, so the LORD has compassion on those who fear him" (Psalm 103:13). Both mothers and fathers, when they hold their baby for the first time or watch the child grow up, have a level of compassion, love, and care for that child.

The Divine Name of God

Yahweh. Jehovah. Adonai. Each of these represent the same divine name for God used in Scripture. Given this . . . why are they so different from one another?

In ancient Israel, the scribes did not typically write out the vowels in Hebrew words. In addition, they did not commonly write the full name of God, out of respect for him. While this may seem odd to English speakers, it was not a problem for the native speakers and readers of the ancient Hebrew language. God's covenantal name was thus written using four Hebrew letters without vowels—*yud-hei-vav-hei*—which is also known as the Tetragrammaton (meaning "four letters.")[9] In English, these four Hebrew letters are translated *YHWH*.

The name *Yahweh* is based on this translation method with the vowels filled in: *YaHWeH*. However, in Latin—the language spoken by the ancient Romans, and the language in which much of the gospel was spread to the world—the Hebrew letters *yud-hei-vav-hei* are translated as *JHVH*. When Bibles began to be translated from Latin into English, the translators also filled in the gaps with vowels, translating God's name as *Jehovah* (*JeHoVaH*).

But what about *Adonai*? As noted above, the ancient Hebrew scribes considered God's divine name to be too sacred to write out or even pronounce. So, when Hebrew vowels were later added to the text, the scribes took the vowels from the word *adonai*, which means "lord" or "master," and placed them between the consonants *yud-hei-vav-hei*. This served as a reminder to the reader not to speak the divine name of God but to instead just say *Adonai*. Most English versions of the Bible follow this practice and translate YHWH as LORD (in small capital or all capital letters).[10]

B. Jehovah is the name *yud-hei-vav-hei*, the four-letter Hebrew name of God pronounced by the Jewish people as *Adonai*. It is the name through which God relates to his people with mercy and compassion.

1. Jehovah showed up in the burning bush and spoke to Moses from the midst of it (see Exodus 3:1–22). The fact that God reveals himself by this name in the burning bush is significant because the Hebrew tells us it's a specific bush—a burning *thorn*bush.

2. Thorns go back to the curse of creation (see Genesis 3:17–19). Thorns are associated with exile, pain, and suffering. Jehovah appearing in the burning bush is God saying, "I have always been with you in your pain and suffering, and I'm with you in your slavery."

3. Jesus is the ultimate embodiment of Jehovah. He hung on a cross made of wood because sin came into the world when we stole from the tree in the Garden of Eden. He had a crown of thorns on his head because he took the curse of creation on himself. He suffered for our sakes.

II. What does the name *Jehovah* reveal about the relationship God wants to have with us?

    A. Jehovah is the name that describes Jesus' work as our Redeemer and Savior. Sin creates a debt that has to be paid. The penalty for breaking God's commandments is death.

        1. God is the God of justice, so the debt *has* to be paid. But if God kept a record of our wrongs, who would be able to stand? So God instead sent Jesus as our Messiah.

        2. When Jesus died on the cross, he satisfied God's justice—the penalty for our sins that had to be paid. But he took the penalty upon himself so that we didn't have to suffer the consequences. This demonstrates his compassion and his mercy toward us.

    B. The prophet Isaiah wrote, "[Jesus] was wounded for our transgressions, He was bruised for our iniquities; the chastisement for our peace was upon Him, and by His stripes we are healed" (Isaiah 53:5 NKJV).

        1. The word *gospel* means good news—and the good news is that God loves us that much. His mercy is not just for those who believe in him and call him Lord. He loves those who mock him still.

2. Jesus said, "I am the way and the truth and the life. No one comes to the Father except through me" (John 14:6). Some people think that is intolerant—but it's actually amazing because it means we can get into heaven. Jesus is the one who did this for us.

III. What does it mean to be people who pursue both God's justice *and* mercy?

A. So many times we identify with God as Elohim—his attribute of strict justice. But we forget that God tempered that justice with compassion . . . with his mercy as *Jehovah*.

1. If we are going to draw people closer to God, we have to embody the balance between justice and mercy. It is the mercy of God that leads people to repentance.

2. The religious leaders of Jesus' day wanted to be like Elohim and just judge the sinner. They wanted Jesus to do the same—to make them repent. But time and again, Jesus gets down on the level of sinners and reaches to those who were considered outcasts.

B. We can't forget that "we love because [Jesus] first loved us" (1 John 4:19).

1. If we don't love others, we are just "a resounding gong or a clanging cymbal" (1 Corinthians 13:1). If we don't love other people, like God loves them, we are just making noise.

Justice *and* Mercy

When God appeared to Moses in the burning thornbush, he revealed himself as the God of mercy (Jehovah), for he was about to deliver his people from slavery. But he also revealed himself as the God of justice (Elohim), because he was also about to judge the Egyptians for the way they had treated the Israelites . . . measure for measure. Perhaps no one embodies this combination of *mercy* and *justice* in the Old Testament better than King David.

In Jewish tradition, a story is told of a rich man who brought a claim against a poor man. In the lawsuit, the rich man claimed that he had the right to the last little sheep that the poor man owned. David was there to adjudicate the matter, and according to the Scriptures and God's Law, he had to rule on behalf of the rich man and award him the poor man's sheep. It was the only way for him to act according to God's justice.

But what about God's *mercy*?

David ultimately ruled in favor of the rich man and said that he deserved the poor man's sheep. But then he paid the fine himself so that the poor man could keep his little sheep. In this way, justice was served to the rich man, while mercy was shown to the poor man.[11]

This is a picture of the justice and mercy that God demonstrated to us. Under the law, we are all guilty of death because of our sins. But God "paid the fine" that we owed through the sacrifice of his Son—"the Lamb of God, who takes away the sin of the world" (John 1:29).

2. Jesus told the religious leaders, "You are like whitewashed tombs, which look beautiful on the outside but on the inside are full of the bones of the dead" (Matthew 23:27). Many of us have no joy and no understanding of the incredible mercy that God has shown to us.

IV. How do we access this kind of mercy from Jehovah?

A. We have to understand that God is a *merciful* father. We can come before him and ask for mercy in our time of need and encounter him on a very personal and real basis.

B. Just as with our own children, God will not abandon us, refuse us, or say he is too busy. We, as fallen parents, feel incredible compassion for our kids when they call out to us. So how much more does our perfect, divine, heavenly parent feel that way about us?

C. Many of us today feel lost, disenfranchised, unseen, and invisible to God. But he is waiting for us to call upon him. God inhabits the praises and prayers of his people (see Psalm 22:3).

D. God wants you to encounter his mercy in the person of Jesus. If you come to him and ask him to reveal himself as the God of compassion—as *Jehovah*—it will bring healing and wholeness to your life and bring you into a whole new relationship with him.

Discuss | 35 minutes

Take some time to discuss what you just watched by answering the following questions. There are some suggested questions below to help you begin your discussion, but feel free to pick any of the additional questions as well as time allows.

Suggested Questions

1. Read Psalm 103:11–18. David compares the greatness of God's mercy to the height of the "the heavens . . . above the earth" (verse 11). How is God revealed as Jehovah in verses 13–18? Which descriptions about God especially stand out to you ?

2. Turn to Exodus 3:1–10. God, for the first time in Scripture, revealed himself in this encounter as *yud-hei-vav-hei*—Jehovah or Adonai, the redeemer. How did God demonstrate that he would live up to this name on behalf of the Israelite people?

3. The fact that God appeared to Moses from a burning thornbush is significant because it refers back to the curse placed against humanity because of Adam and Eve's sin in the Garden of Eden. What was God saying to Moses by appearing *within* the thornbush?

4. The name *Elohim* is associated with God's attribute of strict justice. The name *Jehovah* reveals that God tempered this strict justice with the attribute of mercy. Do you tend to see God more as Elohim (justice) or Jehovah (mercy)? Explain your response.

Additional Questions

5. We are called to be like Christ, but sometimes we are more Elohim than Jehovah. Read Jesus' words on judging others in Matthew 7:1–5. According to this passage, what is the danger in judging others? What should we be doing instead?

6. Jesus' statement reveals that we should be introspective when we consider judging others—that we should first look at *our* actions to see if there are things for which we could be judged. Furthermore, we should forgive as the Lord forgave us (see Colossians 3:13). What are some practical ways that you have learned to temper judging others with mercy?

7. Read Matthew 23:27–28. Why did Jesus compare the Pharisees to whitewashed tombs? What does this say about Jesus' priorities regarding justice and mercy?

8. Justice *matters* to God. What are some ways that God has called you to seek justice for yourself or others? Where has he been calling you to extend more mercy?

Respond | 10 minutes

Review the outline for the video teaching and any notes you took. In the space below, write down your most significant takeaway from this session.

Pray | 10 minutes

End your time by praying together as a group, asking the Lord to help you better understand the aspects of his mercy. Thank your Jehovah Elohim for being both a God of strict justice and tempered mercy. Ask if anyone has any prayer requests to share. Write those requests down in the space below so you and your group members can pray about them in the week ahead.

Name   Request

Personal Study

As you discussed in your group time this week, our God is a God of justice. He cares about the inequalities in our world today and wants us to protect the vulnerable, fight against oppression, and minister to the marginalized of society. But the God we serve is also a God of *mercy*. This is really good news for us, for the Bible states we are all guilty of not living up to God's standards. Given that God's justice requires a penalty to be paid for our transgressions, we are all rightly condemned to death and eternal separation from God. But the Lord, in his mercy, put the penalty that we deserved on his sinless Son. Reflect on this act of grace on God's part as you learn more about his character this week. Once again, be sure to write down your responses to the questions in the spaces provided, as you will be given a few minutes to share your insights at the start of the next session if you are doing this study with others. If you are reading *The God of the Way* alongside this study, first review pages 87–96 in chapter 6 of the book.

— Day 1 —

An Empathetic God

The name *Elohim* represents God as the powerful creator of the world and strict judge, while the second name used for God in the creation story—*Jehovah*—represents his relational side. The Jewish people hold this name so sacred that they don't speak it aloud or spell it out. Instead, when writing it, they use the consonants YHWH. When they read the name aloud from Scripture, they use the name *Adonai*.[12]

This type of reverence for God calls to mind the reverence that Moses demonstrated when he stood before the Lord in the burning bush. He removed his sandals, as he was standing on holy ground (see Exodus 3:5). God revealed himself as Jehovah—a God who had seen the suffering of his people in Egypt and had empathy for them. His great compassion moved him to act by calling on Moses to lead the people out of slavery (see verses 7–9).

Sympathy means to feel sorry for someone, while *empathy* means to get into that person's shoes and feel the same kind of emotions that they are feeling. We don't have to be going through the same circumstances to empathize with another person. If a friend is sad, angry, or anxious, we can empathize with those feelings because we also feel them at times.

While Sympathy distances us from others' pain, empathy brings us closer to those who are suffering. When we empathize with others, we are motivated to act on their behalf. We provide for them in their times of need or simply sit and listen to them. This is why God acts so mercifully toward us. He empathizes with us. He feels *with* us, rather than *for* us. His empathy moves him to act on our behalf, just as he did for the Israelites.

Read | Psalm 147:3–5 and Romans 12:15–18

Reflect

1. The psalmist describes the Lord as one who "heals the brokenhearted and binds up their wounds" (Psalm 147:3). Think about some of the specific times in your life

when you have been brokenhearted. What was the situation? How did God comfort you during that time?

2. As previously mentioned, empathy means to share in the emotions that another person is feeling. How does Paul say that believers in Christ are to empathize with one another? What are we to do if another has wronged us (see Romans 12:15–18)?

3. Think of a time when a friend or loved one truly empathized with you. What did that person do to make it known that he or she understood what you were feeling? How did the empathy you received from that person encourage you at that time?

4. In John's Gospel, when Jesus' friend Lazarus died and he saw his sister Mary weeping, "He groaned in the spirit and was troubled" (John 11:33 NKJV). How easy or difficult is it for you to imagine God being able to empathize with you in this way? What do you think gets in the way of you perceiving God in this manner?

Pray | End your time in prayer. Bring whatever emotions you have before the Lord. Remember, he is your Jehovah! He is able to feel what you feel.

—Day 2—

Christ's Compassion

There is a well-known proverb that states you should "never meet your heroes." If you ever *have* met one of your heroes—a celebrity, coach, or someone you looked up to—you probably know the reason why. Rarely do our heroes live up to the pedestals we've put them on. They fall short of our expectations, because they are human, and disappoint us.

Perhaps the Jewish people of the first century felt the same way when Jesus came along. At the time, their lands were occupied by the Romans, and the religious leaders were expecting the Messiah to come and deliver them as Elohim—the all-mighty creator.[13] They wanted the Messiah to overthrow the throne of Rome and assume that throne for himself. But instead, Jesus came as *Jehovah*. He didn't seek political power and move in the circles of the elite. Rather, he showed compassion to those on the margins. He shared meals with the types of people that most kings or rulers would never have at their banquet tables.

Jesus preached of a different type of kingdom—one in which the meek and poor in spirit were blessed and where the persecuted would receive the kingdom of heaven (see Matthew 5:3–12). He modeled humility and sacrifice rather than power and prestige. He spoke scornfully to the prideful and arrogant and he extended grace and mercy even on the despised tax collectors (see Luke 19:1–10). Jesus taught us to love first and have compassion on the other, especially if we don't understand them (see Matthew 5:43–44).

Jesus was Jehovah in flesh. As he said of his own ministry, "The Spirit of the Lord is on me, because he has anointed me to proclaim good news to the poor. He has sent me to proclaim freedom for the prisoners and recovery of sight for the blind, to set the oppressed free, to proclaim the year of the Lord's favor" (Luke 4:18–19).

Read | Matthew 5:1–10 and Luke 6:20–26

Reflect

1. This passage in Matthew begins what we today call the Sermon on the Mount, so named because it was delivered by Jesus after he "went up on a mountainside and

sat down" to teach the crowds that came to see him (verse 1). What types of people does Jesus say will be blessed in God's kingdom?

2. Biblical scholars believe that Jesus delivered the Sermon on the Mount from a hillside overlooking the Sea of Galilee near Capernaum. This means Jesus' listeners were not among the wealthy elite of society. How do you think they felt about Jesus' words?

3. The passage in Luke represents a parallel narrative called the Sermon on the Plain, so named because it was delivered by Jesus one day "on a level place" when he taught the crowds that came to see him (Luke 6:17). What are some of the similarities between the two accounts? What are some of the differences?

4. Which of the groups in these narratives do you identify with the most? How was God showing mercy to his people by relating to them who is blessed in his sight?

Pray | Spend some time in prayer. Ask God to help you see that you are blessed, in spite of what you might be going through. Ask him to help you see others as blessed and equally deserving of the kingdom of God.

-Day 3-

Never Cancelled

We live in a day and age where "cancel culture" is just a way of life. The term is used to describe a type of ousting of a person from certain professional or social circles—whether that is online, on social media, or in person—due to behaviors that are deemed unacceptable by the most vocal. Those who are ostracized in this way are considered "cancelled."

In this era of cancel culture, it can be all too easy for followers of Christ to get on the bandwagon of "canceling" others for their beliefs, sins, or mistakes. But a quick glance through the Gospels reveals this is not something that Jesus would have done. While he never condoned sin and always proclaimed the truth, he loved people and accepted them where they were in life. Just as he accepts us and loves us in spite of where we are.

Whether you've been a follower of Christ your entire life or you're a new believer, you have probably heard Christians being criticized for being judgmental. Perhaps you've criticized Christians for this. Perhaps you've been criticized for this yourself. It can be tempting, when you learn the Bible and the way of Christ, to feel like you know it all. But this can lead to fundamentalism—a way of thinking that is black-and-white—and cause you to exclude others from your inner circle because they are sinners (or the "wrong type" of sinners).

Jesus was the opposite of a fundamentalist. He exhibited the qualities of compassion and kindness. The one group he did often criticize were the Pharisees—the fundamentalists of Judaism—for thinking they were better than everyone else. Jesus set an example for the church to call people in rather than call them out. We do the same whenever we extend mercy to another person and love them as Christ loved them.

Read | Romans 2:1–4

Reflect

1. In this passage, Paul employs a literary device that was common at the time in which he anticipates a reaction on the part of a reader and refutes those arguments.

How would you describe his tone in this passage? What do you think is motivating his remarks?

2. What does Paul say those who seek to pass judgment on others are actually doing to themselves? What does he say that such people will face (see verses 1–3)?

3. Have you ever felt that you were "cancelled" (whether on social media or in person) because of mistakes that you made? When have you experienced this kind of judgment from others—and how did you react as a result of how you were treated?

4. In what situations do you tend to "pass judgment on someone else" (verse 1) and thus "show contempt for the riches of [God's] kindness" (verse 4)?

Pray | End your time in prayer. Confess any judgmental thoughts you have had toward others this week. Ask Jesus to fill you with love for those you judge most. Have confidence that he—and only he—can change your heart as he reveals the riches of his kindness to you.

Day 4

Made for Relationship

In the previous session, we looked at the beauty of *El* being written into the names of certain biblical characters (such as Elijah, Elisha, Samuel, Israel) and the significance that this holds for us. We worship a God who wants to be near us and who desires for his Spirit to dwell within us (see Romans 8:9). Jesus was the full manifestation of this desire—as he took on flesh and became one of us. The name *Jehovah* emphasizes this relational aspect of God.

However, just as God wants to be in relationship with us, he also wants us to be in relationship with *other people*. When we look at the story of creation, we find that God created the world in twos. Light and darkness. Sea and sky. Man and woman. The first Hebrew letter of the first word in Genesis, the letter *bet*, has a numerical value of two. God created the world (and us) to be in relationship with one another. This is when the world is in perfect alignment.[14]

Think about your own situation. When you are struggling in your relationships with others, how does it affect the rest of your life? When you are lonely and distant from your family, friends, or community, how does it make you feel? We are meant to be in relationship with others, and this is especially true when it comes to our faith. If you've ever been without a church for a period of time, you've probably experienced this. While you can certainly worship God and have spiritual experiences alone, the Lord established a body of believers for a reason. The full expression of our faith is only possible in community—loving others and loving God.

Read | 1 Corinthians 12:12–27

Reflect

1. In this passage, the apostle Paul is speaking to the believers in Corinth about spiritual gifts. Evidently, some in the church were prizing certain gifts above others.

How should the church function as a body made up of many different parts (see verses 12–14)?

2. Paul drives home his point by asking his readers to imagine what would happen if a hand or ear were to decide to no longer be part of the body (see verses 15–16). What is Paul saying to the church about the need to embrace each other's unique gifts?

3. Think about some of the relationships you have formed with other believers in Christ. Which of those relationships have especially encouraged you to grow in your faith?

4. What type of Christian community are you a part of today? How does this community affect your daily life? Or how has the absence of community affected your life?

Pray | Assess your relationships and what types of communities you're in right now. Whether you're craving more friendship or community, desiring restoration for a broken relationship, or feeling grateful for a robust faith community, bring your needs and gratitude before the Lord.

— Day 5 —

Power Revealed

Superheroes often have a secret identity they assume when they are not out saving the world. Batman is Bruce Wayne. Wonder Woman is Diana Prince. Superman is Clark Kent. They all look just like everyone else before they don their suit or cloak and reveal their power.

In a way, we could say that Jesus did the same. He began his ministry in the spirit of Jehovah. He came to earth, took on human form, and for more than thirty years interacted with people in society. Even during his ministry, he often instructed those who saw his power to keep it to themselves (see, for example, Mark 1:41–42).

But Jesus ended his ministry in the spirit of *Elohim*, revealing his power and glory to the world. Jesus was sentenced to death on a cross, and no one survived crucifixion. Jesus' disciples believed that he was dead. The Roman authorities believed that he was dead. His body was carried into a tomb and wrapped in burial clothes. The entrance was sealed with a stone. End of story. But then something unexpected happened.

John describes it this way. Mary Magdalene, one of Jesus' disciples, was standing outside Jesus' empty tomb, weeping because his body was no longer there. She saw a man standing nearby, who she assumed was the gardener. When the man asked why she was crying, she replied, "Sir, if you have carried him away, tell me where you have put him" (John 20:15). It was only when Jesus spoke her name that she recognized him.

Jesus was Jehovah, and he was also Elohim. He had the power to defeat death itself. And not even death can keep us from his power. Because Jesus is our Jehovah Elohim, we can—just like Mary—rejoice that he lives and calls us by name.

Read | Philippians 2:5–11

Reflect

1. In this passage, the apostle Paul describes the mindset that Jesus, the Son of God, had when he came to earth. How does he describe Jesus in verses 6–8?

2. Jesus, even though he was "in very nature God" (verse 6), chose to be "made in human likeness" (verse 7) so that he could interact with us and experience everything that we go through as human beings. But how does Paul then describe Jesus in verses 9–11?

3. Notice at the beginning of this passage that Paul's purpose in describing Jesus' humility is so his readers will have the same mindset in their relationships with each other (see verse 5). What are some of the traits of Jesus that we should model in our friendships?

4. It might be easier for you to think of Jesus as Jehovah, or you might find it easier to think of him as Elohim. What would change about your relationship with Christ if you saw him as *both* fully Jehovah (empathetic and relational) and fully Elohim (all-mighty creator)?

Pray | Spend a few minutes reflecting on this week's personal study time. Did God convict you of anything this week? Did you change in any way? Or learn something new? Talk to God about what you learned this week and what he might be showing you today.

For Next Week

Before you meet again with your group next week, read pages 97–100 in chapter 7 of *The God of the Way*. Also go back and complete any of the study and reflection questions from this personal study that you weren't able to finish.

Schedule

WEEK 3

BEFORE GROUP MEETING	Read pages 97–100 in chapter 7 of *The God of the Way* Read the Welcome section (page 53)
GROUP MEETING	Discuss the Connect questions Watch the video teaching for session 3 Discuss the questions that follow as a group Do the closing exercise and pray (pages 53–64)
PERSONAL STUDY – DAY 1	Complete the daily study (pages 66–67)
PERSONAL STUDY – DAY 2	Complete the daily study (pages 68–69)
PERSONAL STUDY – DAY 3	Complete the daily study (pages 70–71)
PERSONAL STUDY – DAY 4	Complete the daily study (pages 72–73)
PERSONAL STUDY – DAY 5 (before week 4 group meeting)	Complete the daily study (pages 74–75) Read pages 100–102 in chapter 7 in *The God of the Way* Complete any unfinished personal studies

God of Power

אל שדי

EL SHADDAI

[ALL SUFFICIENT GOD]

*Yours, LORD, is the greatness and the power
and the glory and the majesty and the splendor,
for everything in heaven and earth is yours.*

1 CHRONICLES 29:11

Welcome | Read On Your Own

In the last session you learned about Jehovah Elohim, the name for God that reflects how he tempers his strict justice with mercy. Jehovah is the name by which the Lord entered into covenant with his people and the name by which he engages with us. Jesus is the ultimate embodiment of this attribute of God's mercy. He took the penalty on himself for our sins, thus fulfilling God's requirement for justice by suffering and dying in our place.

We learn about these Hebrew names of God—and about God's character, attributes, and nature—through his *Word*. It is the Bible, the written Word of God, that has the power to reveal this knowledge to us. We see the power of God's words in the story of creation. His spoken commands *brought life into existence*. His written Word has the power to do the same!

Perhaps you already know this about God's Word. You've experienced its power and know that life can be "sweeter than honey . . . from the honeycomb" when you follow it (Psalm 19:10). Or perhaps you haven't yet encountered the power of the Word in this way. You are new to studying the Bible and just starting out on your spiritual trek.

Regardless of where you are in the journey, this week's study will help you discover *more* about the power of God's Word. As the apostle Paul wrote, "All Scripture is God-breathed and is useful for teaching, rebuking, correcting and training in righteousness, so that the servant of God may be thoroughly equipped for every good work" (2 Timothy 3:16–17). But even more, the goal is to help you discover more about the *living* Word. For Jesus is the embodiment of God's Word, and he has the power to rescue you, redeem you, and restore you.

Connect | 15 minutes

Welcome to session 3 of *The God of His Word*. To get things started for this week's group time, discuss one of the following questions:

- What is a key insight or takeaway from last week's personal study that you would like to share with the group?

  — *or* —

- How would you describe what your relationship is like with God's Word?

Watch | 20 minutes

Now watch the video for this session. As you watch, use the following outline to record any thoughts or concepts that stand out to you.

I. What can we learn about God's power as revealed in his Word?

    A. God's Word has the power to transform us and the world around us.

        1. The psalmist writes that God's Word is "sweeter than honey" (Psalm 19:10). If unkosher food falls into something that's kosher, it becomes unkosher. The only food that's not true with is honey, because honey has transformative and healing properties.

        2. When we have the "honey" of God's Word in us, it transforms us from the inside out. It gives us an understanding of the nature of God and provides the instructions for life.

    B. The power of God's Word is also key to overcoming the chaos of this world.

        1. "[God] holds everything together with his powerful word" (Hebrews 1:3 NCV). God's Word undergirds all creation. In a sense, it was the blueprint for creation.

Honey in Scripture

"For the LORD your God is bringing you into a good land . . . a land with wheat and barley, vines and fig trees, pomegranates, olive oil and honey" (Deuteronomy 8:7–8).

When we think of honey, we naturally associate it with the sticky substance collected by bees. But in ancient times, honey was also made from the juice of fruits such as grapes, dates, and figs. This could potentially be the type of honey that Moses mentions above, and the type of honey given in other passages where the foods of a land are listed (see 2 Samuel 17:28–29). Whatever its source, the writers of Scripture frequently drew on the sweetness of honey as a metaphor for the good things that God provides—such as God's words (see Psalm 119:103), God's wisdom (see Proverb 24:13–14), and the speech of a friend (see Proverbs 16:24).[15]

Honey from bees might have been rare in Israel (though ancient beehives have been found), but it figures prominently in at least one story. In Judges, we read that Samson killed a lion on his way to visit a woman in the town of Timnah. Some time later, he returned to the town to marry the woman, and on his way he saw that a swarm of bees had set up a hive in the lion's carcass. Samson made up a riddle based on the scene and wagered thirty linen garments and a set of clothes if the other party guessed the answer. Sadly, the situation didn't go well for Samson, and he lost not only the wager but also the woman for his wife (see Judges 14:1–20).[16]

In the New Testament, John the Baptist "wore clothing made of camel's hair, with a leather belt around his waist, and he ate locusts and wild honey" (Mark 1:6). John's food and clothing emphasize that he was living off the land and was completely dedicated to God's purposes.[17] Finally, in the book of Revelation, an angel gave John a scroll to eat, saying it "will turn your stomach sour, but 'in your mouth it will be as sweet as honey'" (Revelation 10:9). For John, receiving the Word of God brought "sweetness" and joy, but it also resulted in the unpleasant experience of having to proclaim a message of judgment and woe.[18]

2. When God creates the heavens and earth, his words form the "code" for the spiritual laws of our world. The numeric values behind those words form the numeric code of creation.

C. Just as there are physical laws, there are spiritual laws. When we break the spiritual laws that are woven into creation itself, it brings chaos into the world.

   1. This is what happened with the Fall. It's almost like sin is a virus in the code of creation. But when we honor God's Word, it brings order, life, and blessing.

   2. God's power is revealed through the written Word and also the *living* Word. When Jesus returns and fulfills everything in the written Word, all the world will be transformed.

II. What is the significance of God creating the world through ten utterances?

A. God speaks the world into existence through *ten* utterances (see Genesis 1). God also delivers his people out under Moses by speaking *ten* plagues against the Egyptians.

   1. Pharaoh didn't obey when God sent Moses to speak his Word. The ten plagues are actually an undoing of the very creative order God established in the beginning.

2. When Pharaoh disobeyed the Lord, the Egyptians experienced chaos out of order. God's Word is woven into the fabric of creation. When we disregard God's Word, the result is chaos and upheaval.

3. The Hebrew word for "formless and void" (*tohu vavohu*) has a numerical value of 430, all Egypt has a numerical value of 430, and Israel was in slavery for 430 years. Ultimately, God brought Israel out of Egypt at the end of those 430 years to restore order.

B. The number ten is also connected to the power of God's word to bring about new creation.

1. The Ten Commandments that God gave to Moses were meant to reverse the chaos that Israel experienced in Egypt. Just as God spoke ten times at creation, he speaks the Ten Commandments to bring about *new* creation—a transformation in his people's lives.

2. The Israelites suffered in exile for 430 years. It was in the 430th year that God brought them out of Egypt and gave them the Ten Commandments—his Word—at Mount Sinai.

III. What is the significance of Jesus as the Living Word as it relates to God's power over chaos?

  A. The prophet Micah wrote that the Messiah would come from Bethlehem Ephrathah and that his goings forth "are from long ago, from the days of eternity" (Micah 5:2 NASB).

   1. The expression "from the days of eternity" in Hebrew has a numerical value of 430. Not only is it God's Word that helps us overcome chaos, but it is also the *living* Word, the Messiah, who helps us overcome chaos.

   2. When Jesus died, there were three hours of darkness. This ties to the three days of darkness in Egypt, because Jesus is the "greater . . . than Moses" (Hebrews 3:3). It also ties to the ninth plague, the death of the firstborn, for this was the death of God's son.

  B. It goes back even further, because God created the world out of darkness. Darkness is what existed before the world ever began.

   1. In a sense, Jesus is going back to before the world began—when it was in a state of chaos. Only the one who existed before the chaos existed can reverse that chaos and bring back the light.

   2. God's power is on full display in our lives and in what he wants to do in our lives. There are so many mysteries in God's Word . . . and we can always go deeper!

Undoing Order

When God spoke the world into existence—creating *order* out of *chaos*—he did so through ten spoken commands. Later, God sent Moses to Pharaoh to command him to free the Israelites, but Pharoah refused to heed these commands. As a result, God issued ten plagues that represented an undoing of the order that had been established at creation. The following shows the parallel between God's commands at creation and the ten plagues.[19]

Plague Against Egypt	Command at Creation
Nile River turned to blood (Exodus 7:14–24)	Creation of the seas (Genesis 1:9–10)
Frogs emerge from the Nile (Exodus 8:1–15)	Creation of sea creatures (Genesis 1:20–23)
Gnats emerge from the dust of the ground in Egypt ((Exodus 8:1–19)	Creation of animals that move along the ground (Genesis 1:24–25)
Flies fill the air of Egypt (Exodus 8:20–32)	Creation of flying creatures (Genesis 1:20–23)
Pestilence against livestock (Exodus 9:1–7)	Creation of livestock (Genesis 1:24–25)
Boils on animals and people (Exodus 9:8–12)	Creation of animals and people (Genesis 1:24–26)
Hail destroys plants (Exodus 9:13–35)	Creation of plants (Genesis 1:11–13)
Locusts devour plants (Exodus 10:1–20)	Creation of plants (Genesis 1:11–13)
Darkness over the land (Exodus 10:21–29)	Light over the void (Genesis 1:3–5)
Death of the Firstborn	Creation of people (Genesis 1:27–30)

C. One of the ways we can go deeper is by looking at the word *redemption*.

    1. In Hebrew, the word for redemption is *geulah*, while the Hebrew word for exile is *golah*. There is only one letter difference in *exile* and *redemption*, and it's the letter *aleph*.

    2. *Aleph* is the letter that represents the name of God and has a numerical value of one. It points to God's oneness—that he alone is the creator and the redeemer.

    3. When you take the *aleph* out of the word for *redemption*, you are left with exile. Exile is about disconnection and distance from God.

IV. What is the type of redemption that God's power brings to us through Christ?

    A. God gave us his written Word, but it took the *living* Word—Yeshua Jesus—to come in the flesh (see John 1:1–3, 14), fulfill everything the Word had spoken of, and bring redemption and salvation.

    B. The Hebrew word for redemption (*geulah*) means to redeem in such a way that it elevates the person to another level. The redemption that Jesus brings elevates every aspect of our lives.

C. If we want to know what God is like, how we should love people, and know what it's like to live for God, we need only look to Jesus, for he is the fullness of what the Scriptures say.

Discuss | 35 minutes

Take some time to discuss what you just watched by answering the following questions. There are some suggested questions below to help you begin your discussion, but feel free to pick any of the additional questions as well as time allows.

Suggested Questions

1. The psalmist wrote that God's Word is "sweeter than honey" (Psalm 19:10). From a Jewish perspective, if a piece of unkosher food falls into something kosher, that food becomes *unkosher*. Honey is an exception because of its transformative properties. How does this imagery relate to the power that God's Word can have in our lives?

2. When God sent Moses to Pharoah to speak his word, the Egyptian ruler refused to obey, resulting in the ten plagues (see Exodus 7:1–5). The ten plagues were an undoing of the creative order that God had established in the beginning. What does this reveal about the power of God's Word? What does God's Word have the power to do?

3. God spoke ten commands that brought the world into existence (see Genesis 1). He later led the Israelites to the foot of Mount Sinai and gave the Ten Commandments to Moses (see Exodus 20:1–17). What is the connection between the two as it relates to the restorative work that God wanted to do in his people's lives?

4. The Gospels reveal that darkness covered the land for three hours as Jesus hung on the cross (see Luke 23:44). What does this darkness represent? What was Jesus— the one who existed before the world began—restoring in this moment?

Additional Questions

5. Read Hebrews 4:12–13. What does this passage say about God's Word? What are some of the functions of the Word of God as it relates to shaping our lives?

6. The Hebrew word for redemption is *geulah*, while the Hebrew word for exile is *golah*. There is only one letter difference between the two, and it's the letter *aleph*—the letter that represents God. What happens when God (*aleph*) is removed from our lives?

7. How does studying the Hebrew translations and the numerical value of certain words and their symbolism affect your view of Scripture, its depth, and its purpose in your life?

8. Jesus is the living Word of God and has the power to bring order out chaos. What is a situation in your life today where you need the power of the living Word to restore order?

Respond | 10 minutes

Review the outline for the video teaching and any notes you took. In the space below, write down your most significant takeaway from this session.

Pray | 10 minutes

End your time by praying together as a group, asking God to speak to you through his Word and reveal his power. Ask if anyone has any prayer requests to share. Write those requests down in the space below so you and your group members can pray about them in the week ahead.

Name	Request

Personal Study

As you discussed in your group time this week, our God is a God of power. At the dawn of creation, the Lord commanded there to be light, sky, land, plants, the sun, the moon, animals, and humans, and these things came into existence through the power of his words. God created order out of chaos when crafting the world, and he is still bringing order out of chaos when it comes to crafting our lives. Our sin creates a state of exile between us and God—just like Adam and Eve experienced when they were exiled from the Garden—but the Lord, in his great mercy, sent Jesus into the world to redeem us. Reflect on these aspects of his power as you go through the study this week. Once again, write down your responses to the questions in the spaces provided, as you will be given a few minutes to share your insights at the start of the next session if you are doing this study with others. If you are reading *The God of the Way* alongside this study, first review pages 97–100 in chapter 7 of the book.

—Day 1—

Sweeter than Honey

Think about a book you loved when you were young. What was the story? Why did you like it? If you were to read that book today, how would you feel about it? Would you still find the story to be captivating? Or do you think—now that you have read many more books over your lifetime—that you would find the plot to be predictable and mundane? Our relationship with stories and characters changes over time. Maybe we still love them. Maybe not so much. As we change, so does the way we view stories and tales from our past.

Our relationship with God's Word also changes as we go through life. Think about the first time that you read the Bible. How did you feel about it? What were some of the stories that captivated your imagination? How did you respond to its teachings? Did you find any parts of God's Word too challenging to comprehend? Now think about how you read the Bible today. What stories resonate with you? What questions do you have? What do you find comforting and what do you find confusing? As we change, so does our relationship with God's Word.

In the psalm you will read today, the author uses words such as *precepts*, *commandment*, and *rules* to refer to his version of God's Word, the Torah, which are the first five books of the Old Testament that include God's law to the Israelites. This is what the psalmist would have known and loved. He didn't have the Gospels or all the epistles that we have in our Bibles today, but still, the Scripture that he knew was powerful to him. Use today's study time to likewise take an assessment of your relationship with God's Word. Be honest with yourself. It's okay if your relationship with the Bible looks different than it once did.

Read | Psalm 19:8–11

Reflect

1. The psalmist lists not only a few truths about God's Word but also the impact that those truths have had on him personally. What does he say about the precepts, the

commands, and the decrees of the Lord? What does he say about the fear of the Lord (see verses 8–9)?

2. What are some of the benefits the psalmist lists for those who follow God's precepts, commands, and decrees, and show honor and respect to him (see verses 8–9)?

3. From a Jewish perspective, honey has such transformative and healing powers that if something unkosher (not prepared according to Jewish law) falls into it, that food becomes kosher. In what ways is this like the power of God's Word (see verse 10)?

4. The psalmist considered God's Word to be "more precious than gold" (verse 10). How would you describe the way that you feel about God's Word?

Pray | Take some time to mediate on this passage. Read it aloud several times. If a verse stands out, spend some time with it. Ask God what he might be revealing to you through this psalm.

— Day 2 —

Spoken, Written, Living

The phrase "word of God" or "word of the Lord" has a number of different meanings in the Bible. Sometimes, it refers to God *speaking* actual words and issuing spoken commands. Other times, it refers to the words that God gave to certain people, who then *wrote* them down in what we know as the Bible. Jesus is also referred to as "the Word." He represents the *living* embodiment of God's word to us. The Lord has chosen to reveal his power to us in these ways—through his *spoken* word, *written* word, and *living* word.

We encounter the power of God's *spoken* word in the story of creation. Again and again, Gpd speaks and brings order out of the chaos. "God said, 'Let there be light'; and there was light. . . . God said, 'Let there be an expanse in the midst of the waters, and let it separate the waters from the waters.' . . . God said, 'Let the waters below the heavens be gathered into one place, and let the dry land appear' " (Genesis 1:3, 6, 9 NASB).

We encounter the power of God's *written* word in the story of God giving the Ten Commandments to Moses on the summit of Mount Sinai: "The LORD said to Moses, 'Come up to me on the mountain and stay here, and I will give you the tablets of stone with the law and commandments I have written for their instruction' " (Exodus 24:12).

We encounter the power of the *living* word in the incarnation: "In the beginning was the Word, and the Word was with God, and the Word was God. He was with God in the beginning. Through him all things were made; without him nothing was made that has been made. In him was life, and that life was the light of all mankind" (John 1:1-4). God's word creates life, creates law, and—in Christ—creates a way for us to forever be with God.

Read | Isaiah 40:3–8

Reflect

1. The prophet Isaiah describes the "voice of one calling" who will tell the people to "prepare the way for the LORD" (verse 3). This prophecy was fulfilled in John the

Baptist, who later prepared the people for the coming of Christ (see John 1:23). What does the prophet Isaiah say will happen at the coming of Jesus, the Messiah (see Isaiah 40:4–5)?

2. Why will God choose to reveal his glory to people (see verse 5)?

3. Isaiah writes that all things eventually fade away—"the grass withers and the flowers fall" (verse 7). But what endures forever? Why do you think this is (see verse 8)?

4. What revelation of God's word do you connect with the best—God's written word, God's spoken word to you, or Jesus as the Word? Explain your response.

Pray | End your time in prayer. Thank God for revealing his spoken, written, and living word to you. Ask him to continue to reveal his will for your life as you encounter him today.

— Day 3 —

A Hard Heart

Our world today is governed by *rules*. There are rules we have to follow at work. There are rules we have to adhere to at home and at school. There are rules we have to follow when we are out driving around on the road. Rules are established to keep people in line and let them know what the consequences will be if they are broken.

We might be tempted to think that God's Word has the same sole purpose—to keep us in line and let us know what the consequences will be if we fail. Certainly, the Bible does reveal God's rules for living and lets us know the blessings we will receive when we obey the Lord and the consequences we will endure when we go our own way (see Deuteronomy 28). But God's Word does not only impact our *external* actions. When we disobey what God says, the greatest impact is on what happens *internally*—what happens inside our hearts.

Consider the case of Pharoah in the story of the Exodus. Pharaoh was instructed to obey God and let the Israelites go. But he replied, "Who is the LORD, that I should obey him and let Israel go? I do not know the LORD and I will not let Israel go" (Exodus 5:2). Pharaoh's heart is described as "unyielding" (7:14). As a result, God sent plagues on the Egyptians.

God gave Pharaoh multiple opportunities to soften his heart and change his ways. But with each plague, Pharoah's heart instead "became hard," and he "hardened his heart" (7:22; 8:32). Pharaoh's hard heart was the reason why he disobeyed God, and it was a consequence of disobeying God. While ignoring God's word on occasion may seem innocent enough, these moments add up, affecting our hearts toward God and his word. The more we ignore God's word, the harder our hearts become.

Read | Matthew 13:10–15

Reflect

1. Jesus often taught the people using short stories (which we today call *parables*) that illuminated certain truths about the message he was proclaiming. One time, the

disciples asked Jesus why he taught this way. What response did Jesus give to them (see verses 10–13)?

2. Jesus goes on to quote a passage from the prophet Isaiah to explain the people's condition to his disciples and reveal why he must teach them using parables. What does Jesus say are the consequences of a "calloused" heart (see verse 15)?

3. Jesus says the people of his day could "hardly hear with their ears" and had "closed their eyes" to the truths of God's kingdom. Think about your own life. When was a time when your heart was hard toward God and closed off to what he had to say?

4. How would you describe the state of your heart toward God and his Word today? Are you open to it or closed off? Explain your response.

Pray | End your time in prayer. Ask God to show any areas in your life where your heart has become hardened toward him. Ask him to open your eyes and your ears to his Word.

— Day 4 —

A Heart of Flesh

The Israelites had a long history of obeying God and then disobeying him. The pattern began back in the Exodus when the people formed into a nation under Moses. They obeyed God at times . . . but were also prone to grumble and disobey (see Exodus 17:3; 32:7). The pattern continued when the Israelites were in the promised land during the time of the judges. When the nation became a monarchy, some of the kings followed God . . . but most did not.

Seasons of faithfulness were followed by seasons of rebellion. Because of this, the Israelites' history was tumultuous—claiming God's victory one day and suffering defeat the next. Maybe you can relate. Your own relationship with God is marked with times of faithfulness and times of disobedience, rebellion, or apathy. You've been in the desert, and you've been on the mountain. Your heart has been hard to his Word, and it has been soft.

One of the Israelites' most heartbreaking defeats occurred when they were conquered by the Babylonians, taken away from their native land of Judah, and forced to live in captivity. The Old Testament is filled with laments about this period in their history. But it is also filled with passages of hope. Even though the people were in captivity, prophets such as Ezekiel, whom you'll read below, proclaimed good news. Israel would return to God's favor. They would right their ways. They would obey God again and prosper in the land he promised them.

You might need this promise today. Maybe, just like the Israelites, you've been on a long and hard road with God that has not always been smooth. Fortunately, God is in the business of changing hearts! His word can make a heart of stone turn into flesh again.

Read | Ezekiel 11:17–20

Reflect

1. God promised his people in exile that he would gather them back together from the nations where they had been scattered and return the land of Israel to them

(see verse 17). What does the Lord say will happen once his people are back in that land (see verses 18–19)?

2. God promises to give his people "an undivided heart" and put "a new spirit in them" (verse 19). What will this new heart of flesh allow them to do (see verse 20)?

3. Has God's Word ever softened your heart toward something or someone? If so, how?

4. King David prayed, "Create in me a pure heart, O God, and renew a steadfast spirit within me" (Psalm 51:10). What is an area of your life where you need a new heart?

Pray | Spend a few moments in prayer. Ask God to give you what he promised the Israelites: a heart of flesh and a new spirit. Thank him for the work that he has already done in your life.

— Day 5 —

A New Creation

When John called Jesus "the Word," the Greek word he used was *logos*, which can mean "spoken word," "reason," or "plan."[20] In using *logos*, John was explaining the nature of Jesus' relationship to God and to us: "In the beginning was the Word, and the Word was with God, and the Word was God. He was with God in the beginning. Through him all things were made; without him nothing was made that has been made" (John 1:1–3).

We know from the story of creation that God's spoken word brought the world into existence (see Genesis 1). John is stating in this passage that Jesus was present with God at the time of creation. But even more, Jesus was the one responsible for making it happen—the *logos* of God. As one scholar notes, "Jesus is the physical manifestation of God the Father, just as a spoken word is the physical manifestation of our inner thoughts. Until Jesus took action and created the universe, there was no physical reality to God's presence. But when God 'spoke' (*i.e.,* when Jesus took action), the Creation came into existence."[21]

Jesus played a vital role in the creation of the earth. But he also plays a vital role in bringing out the new creation within us. As the apostle Paul said of his own life, "I have been crucified with Christ and I no longer live, but Christ lives in me. The life I now live in the body, I live by faith in the Son of God, who loved me and gave himself for me" (Galatians 2:20). Jesus was capable of bringing life in existence, and he is capable of bringing *new* life in you.

Read | 2 Corinthians: 5:10–21

Reflect

1. In this passage, Paul states that a transformation must take place when we put our faith in Christ: "[Jesus] died for all, that those who live should no longer live for themselves but for him who died for them and was raised again" (verse 15). What kind of changes should take place in a person who has chosen to follow Christ (see verses 16–17)?

2. Paul writes, "All this is from God, who reconciled us to himself through Christ" (verse 18). What does it mean that we have been given the "message of reconciliation"? What does Jesus instruct us to do as his "ambassadors" (verses 19–20)?

3. Paul writes that "the old has gone, the new is here" (verse 17). Is there anything from your past that you are having difficulty in letting go—either a pattern of sin or shame you feel because of that past sin? What transformation do you need from Christ today?

4. What would it look like for you to really believe that you are a *new* creation in Christ— that your past sins are not counted against you and you can truly change?

Pray | Spend a few minutes reflecting on this week's personal study time. Did God convict you of anything this week? Did you change in any way? Or learn something new? Talk to God about what you learned this week and what he might be showing you today.

For Next Week

Before you meet again with your group next week, read pages 100–102 in chapter 7 of *The God of the Way*. Also go back and complete any of the study and reflection questions from this personal study that you weren't able to finish.

WEEK 4

BEFORE GROUP MEETING	Read pages 100–102 in chapter 7 of *The God of the Way* Read the Welcome section (page 79)
GROUP MEETING	Discuss the Connect questions Watch the video teaching for session 4 Discuss the questions that follow as a group Do the closing exercise and pray (pages 79–90)
PERSONAL STUDY – DAY 1	Complete the daily study (pages 92–93)
PERSONAL STUDY – DAY 2	Complete the daily study (pages 94–95)
PERSONAL STUDY – DAY 3	Complete the daily study (pages 96–97)
PERSONAL STUDY – DAY 4	Complete the daily study (pages 98–99)
PERSONAL STUDY – DAY 5 (before week 5 group meeting)	Complete the daily study (pages 100–101) Read pages 102–107 in chapter 7 in *The God of the Way* Complete any unfinished personal studies

God of Wisdom

אל דעות

EL DEAH

[ALL KNOWING GOD]

The LORD gives wisdom;
from his mouth come knowledge and understanding.

PROVERBS 2:6

Welcome | Read On Your Own

In the last session, you learned about the power of God's Word. Whether it is God's spoken word, his written Word, or Jesus as the living Word, God has the power to create and bring order to chaos. A part of this power is the way the Word can bring us wisdom.

Wisdom is not a sought-after commodity in our culture. We tend to be more interested in status, money, and celebrity. We follow influencers on social media not because they are wise but because they are beautiful, successful, and have perfectly curated feeds. But according to Scripture, wisdom is something we should seek all the days of our lives, for "wisdom is more precious than rubies, and nothing you desire can compare with her" (Proverbs 8:11).

In this session, you will learn about the wisdom of God and how it was present even during creation. You will explore how God's Word imparts wisdom and encourages you to seek the ways of God above all else. You will discover that wisdom will keep you in step with God's will. When you are wise, you follow him. When you are unwise, you follow everything else—friends, family members, influencers, politicians . . . to name just a few. You will also explore how Jesus sought wisdom from God and continued to grow in it.

This is the beauty of wisdom. You can always accumulate more of it over the course of your life! Just think about when you were in your twenties, thirties, or forties. You probably thought you were wise then, but in hindsight, you see that you had a lot of learning to do. Fortunately, you have a text available to you that offers endless wisdom. If you want to know how to be wise, you can go to straight to wisdom's source: God's Word.

Connect | 15 minutes

Welcome to session 4 of *The God of His Word*. To get things started for this week's group time, discuss one of the following questions:

- What is a key insight or takeaway from last week's personal study that you would like to share with the group?

  — *or* —

- When you need to make a major decision about what to do next in your life, where do you typically go for wisdom?

Watch | 20 minutes

Now watch the video for this session. As you watch, use the following outline to record any thoughts or concepts that stand out to you.

I. How do we encounter the God of wisdom?

    A. The God of wisdom is found in his Word. There is wisdom to be found in the Word of God that is available to each and every one of us!

        1. God's Word is the blueprint for creation. It contains the divine design for our lives. When we walk in that wisdom, and understand God's design for us, then creation works for us.

        2. When we work the Word . . . the Word works for us. The apostle Paul writes that the Word of God has the power to transform us and renew our minds (see Romans 12:2).

    B. The wisdom God reveals in his Word can cut away the parts of us that are not good.

        1. God's Word has the power to sculpt us and shape us. It can make us into something better—into something more beautiful—that better resembles the image of God.

Rooted in God's Word

"The LORD would speak to Moses face to face, as one speaks to a friend. Then Moses would return to the camp, but his young aide Joshua son of Nun did not leave the tent" (Exodus 33:11).

Joshua had learned the value of abiding in God's presence and meditating on God's Word. He would accompany Moses when he went into the tent of meeting . . . and linger there for a while. Later, when God called on Joshua to lead the people into the promised land, the Lord encouraged him to "keep this Book of the Law always on your lips; meditate on it day and night, so that you may be careful to do everything written in it" (Joshua 1:8).

It is so important for us to likewise spend time with God each day and meditate on his Word. As the psalmist declared, "I am like an olive tree flourishing in the house of God" (Psalm 52:8). If we want to flourish in our relationship with God, we have to take the time to abide in his presence and listen to his voice. We need to meditate on God's Word each day so that we will be like a "tree planted by streams of water, which yields its fruit in season and whose leaf does not wither—whatever they do prospers" (Psalm 1:3).

When we are rooted in God's Word—and those roots run deep—we won't be blown over when the winds of testing come. Instead, we will stand firm, flourish, and bear good fruit. But if we want that to happen, we have to follow the example of Joshua and regularly plant the seeds of God's Word into our heart. We have to spend time each day in the presence of the Master Gardener, listening to his instruction and wisdom on how to help that seed grow.

2. Meditating on God's Word is important. "[The one] who meditates on his law day and night . . . is like a tree planted by streams of water, which yields its fruit in season and whose leaf does not wither—whatever they do prospers" (Psalm 1:2–3).

II. How does God reveal his wisdom to us?

A. If we ask God for wisdom, he will liberally provide it to us (see James 1:5). Wisdom goes back to creation itself: "In the beginning God created the heavens and the earth" (Genesis 1:1).

1. The Hebrew word for "in the beginning" (*bereisheet*) can also be translated "through the first." So this verse can be read, "Through the first God created the heavens and the earth."

2. The book of Proverbs states that there is a "beginning of wisdom" (4:7). The rabbis interpret Genesis 1:1 as God creating the world in the beginning through the wisdom of God's Word.

B. Even Jesus "grew in wisdom and stature, and in favor with God and man" (Luke 2:52).

    1. Jesus, the Son of God, had to grow in wisdom and stature. This verse also reveals that whenever there is an increase in wisdom, there is an increase of favor on our lives.

    2. So many people are looking to the world for wisdom. But God's Word contains the eternal and timeless wisdom that we need!

III. What is required on our part for God to fill us with his wisdom?

A. An example of what is required to receive wisdom can be found in the example of the Dead Sea. It is fed by the Jordan River, the same river that feeds the Sea of Galilee.

    1. The Sea of Galilee is teaming with life, but there is nothing of consequence living in the Dead Sea. The Dead Sea *receives* from the Jordan River without *giving* it out.

    2. We just ask God to bless us with wisdom. We have to be willing to share that wisdom and be a blessing in the lives of others. When we don't give, we become as dead as the Dead Sea.

B. We are not just called to *save* souls . . . we are also called to *make* souls.

   1. We are to help people become disciples of Christ, which means sharing the wisdom of the Scriptures with them so that they can be conformed into the image and the likeness of Christ.

   2. It's like when a mother gives birth to a baby. The birthing is just the first *part* of the process. What follows is a lifetime of imparting wisdom and guidance to the child.

IV. How does God reveal his wisdom through Jesus, the living Word?

   A. God's wisdom is revealed in the person of Jesus. He said of himself, "A greater than Solomon is here" (Matthew 12:42 NKJV). We see Jesus demonstrate this wisdom in practical ways.

   1. There is a "Solomon moment" in Scripture where a woman caught in adultery is brought to Jesus (see John 8:1–11). He knows the religious leaders are just trying to make him look bad so they can condemn him. He needs divine wisdom to navigate the situation.

Living Water in the Dead Sea

"This water flows toward the eastern region and goes down into the Arabah, where it enters the Dead Sea. When it empties into the sea, the salty water there becomes fresh. Swarms of living creatures will live wherever the river flows" (Ezekiel 47:8–9).

The Dead Sea is so salty that no significant life can exist in its waters. But this prophecy reveals that the Dead Sea won't *stay* dead. Living water will flow from the throne of the Messiah into the Dead Sea, and it will be made alive. In fact, it will teem with such "large numbers of fish" that "fishermen will stand along the shore . . . spreading nets" (verses 9–10).

Researchers are providing us with a sneak preview of this reality. Freshwater springs have been discovered on the floor of the Dead Sea—and with these springs, a bit of life is returning. As one scientist commented, "While there are no fish present, carpets of microorganisms that cover large seafloor areas contain considerable richness of species."[22]

2. Jesus gets down on the woman's level. Everyone else is looking over her, condemning her, shaking their fist at her, and judging her. But Jesus gets on her level and writes in the dirt.

B. The Bible records that Jesus takes his finger and writes *twice* in the dirt. This a significant detail that we often miss.

1. There are two times in Scripture that the finger of God is mentioned. The first is when the Israelites are in Egypt. The Egyptian sorcerers see the plagues and say, "This is the finger of God" (Exodus 8:19). These sorcerers acknowledge God's power and that he is bringing redemption to his people.

2. The second time is when God writes the Ten Commandments with his own finger (see Deuteronomy 9:10). When Moses comes down to show them what was written, he finds the Israelites committing idolatry by worshiping the golden calf (see Exodus 32:1–8).

3. We don't know what Jesus wrote in the ground, but whatever it was, the religious leaders understood what the finger of God meant. They were so convicted that they walked away, leaving just Jesus and the woman behind (see John 8:9). This is wisdom.

C. This woman was forever changed when she encountered the living Word and she received the words of life from him. This is what God's Word does in our lives. It never looks down on us. God's Word might convict us at times, but it never condemns us.

Discuss | 35 minutes

Take some time to discuss what you just watched by answering the following questions. There are some suggested questions below to help you begin your discussion, but feel free to pick any of the additional questions as well as time allows.

Suggested Questions

1. As mentioned in the teaching, the rabbis make a connection between Genesis 1:1 (the beginning of creation) and Proverbs 4:7 (the beginning of wisdom). The conclusion they reach is that God created the heavens and the earth *through the wisdom of God's Word*. What does this imply about the importance of wisdom in our lives?

2. Read Proverbs 4:5–9. This passage is written in the form of a father giving instruction to his sons (see verse 1). What does this "father" say that wisdom will do in their lives (see verse 6)? What will happen if they cherish and embrace wisdom (see verse 8)?

3. According to Psalm 1:3, a person who meditates on God's Word is "like a tree planted by streams of water." What does this imply about the person who is rooted in God's Word? What is some of the fruit that you have seen in your life because of being "planted" in God's Word?

4. Read John 8:1–11. Jesus understood the religious leaders were bringing this woman to him not because of anything that she had done but because they were trying to trap him and condemn him. How did Jesus show wisdom in this situation? What does this story reveal about the power of wisdom and how it should be used?

Additional Questions

5. Read Philippians 1:4–6. We often focus on salvation as the end goal of Christianity when it is actually just the beginning. What is the "good work" that Paul mentions in this passage? What role does wisdom play in progressing in our faith?

6. In Jewish thought, there is an "upper" wisdom and a "lower" wisdom. What is the difference between the two? Why is it so tempting to rely on lower wisdom?

7. Read Matthew 28:19–20. The disciples of Jesus had benefited from his wisdom during his time on earth, but now the Lord had a special commission for them. What did Jesus instruct them to do with what they had learned? How does this apply to us today?

8. Think about the example given of the Dead Sea. Fresh water flows in from the Jordan River, but with no outlet for that water, it stagnates and loses its life-giving properties. How is this similar to what happens when wisdom is not shared?

Respond | 10 minutes

Review the outline for the video teaching and any notes you took. In the space below, write down your most significant takeaway from this session.

Pray | 10 minutes

End your time by praying together as a group, asking the Lord to give you his divine wisdom as you study his Word. Ask if anyone has any prayer requests to share. Write those requests down in the space below so you and your group members can pray about them in the week ahead.

Name   Request

Personal Study

As you discussed in your group time this week, our God is a God of wisdom. We access that wisdom through his Word, which serves as the blueprint for our lives. When we work the Word . . . the Word works for us! It has the power to sculpt and shape our attitudes, actions, and beliefs as we soak in the wisdom that God pours over us. It has the power to cut away any false beliefs and perceptions that we have picked up over the years. God's wisdom in his Word can help us to become more like Christ and reflect his goodness to the world. Reflect on these truths as you study God's Word this week. Be sure to write down your responses to the questions in the spaces provided, as you will be given a few minutes to share your insights at the start of the next session if you are doing this study with others. If you are reading *The God of the Way* alongside this study, first review pages 97–100 in chapter 7 of the book.

-Day 1-

Wisdom Never Fails

What comes to your mind when you hear the word *wisdom*? Perhaps you picture an elderly, grey-haired, bespectacled grandfather who is kindly instructing you on the lessons that he learned in life. Maybe the image of a professor or pastor comes to mind. Maybe the word feels weighty to you—something you want but don't yet know how to get. Or maybe the word is a turn-off. All of the seemingly wise people in your life—your parents, mentors, and others—all let you down. You just don't find value in wisdom as you once did.

Wisdom—seeking it and finding it—is a theme that runs throughout the pages of Scripture. There's even an entire section of the Old Testament—the books of Proverbs, Job, and Ecclesiastes—that is known as the "wisdom literature." These books focus on the wisdom that comes from God. But as you learned in this week's teaching, *wisdom* appears in Scripture as early as Genesis 1:1. The Hebrew word *bereisheet*, which is typically translated in English Bibles as "in the beginning," is associated with "God creating the world through wisdom and understanding."[23]

Just as the Lord created the world through wisdom, bringing beautiful things into existence as they responded to his voice, so he creates new and beautiful things within you as you respond to the wisdom in his Word. While the seemingly wise people in your life might have failed you in the past, you have the promise that "no word from God will ever fail" (Luke 1:37). What's more, that wisdom is *always* available to you. As James wrote, "If any of you lacks wisdom, you should ask God, who gives generously to all without finding fault, and it will be given to you" (1:5).

Read | Proverbs 8:7–18

Reflect

1. The author of this passage personifies wisdom as a woman who is speaking "what is true" and whose "words . . . are just" (verse 7). What does this "woman" who is

personified as wisdom say about the value of her words? Why should we choose wisdom over worldly riches (see verses 9–11)?

2. The author writes, "I, wisdom, dwell together with prudence" (verse 12). How do you define *prudence*? Why do these two qualities go hand in hand?

3. Wisdom and prudence grant their recipients valuable benefits: "By me kings reign and rulers issue decrees that are just; by me princes govern, and nobles—all who rule on earth" (verses 15–16). What is required to receive these benefits (see verses 17–18)?

4. God's Word contains God's wisdom and his divine design for your life. Where do you especially need his wisdom in your life right now?

Pray | End your time by asking God to grant you his wisdom. Claim the promise that he will generously give it to you without finding fault. Commit to acting on the instruction he provides.

-Day 2-
Seeking Wisdom

Google, Siri, and Alexa have all become our go-tos for questions about the weather, traffic, and general trivia. We trust these sources . . . even if that trust is a bit blind. (After all, we can't trust *everything* we read online.) But what do we do with our *big* questions? It's great to have an app that immediately tells us there is no rain in the forecast and reveals the name of that song stuck in our head. But it is much more difficult to instantly know what we should do about our jobs, our health, our relationships—and our lives in general. Wisdom is a *pursuit*.

You can't just type a random question in the Bible and get the exact answer you are seeking. Wisdom has to be sought. As the psalmist wrote, "I have hidden your word in my heart that I might not sin against you" (Psalm 119:11). You can't hide something in your heart that you haven't yet discovered. Or as Paul wrote, "Do your best to present yourself to God as one approved, a worker who does not need to be ashamed and who correctly handles the word of truth" (2 Timothy 2:15). You can't correctly handle truth if you don't know what the truth is.

Wisdom calls out to you (see Proverbs 8:1). But *you* have to answer her call. You do this by what you are doing right now—opening up your Bible to study what it has to say. The Lord may not reveal a specific answer to a specific question that you have (though he might). But he will guide you to what he wants you to learn about his nature, his care for you, his ability to handle any problems in your future, and why you can always depend on him. The more you dwell on God's Word, the more wisdom he will instill in you. And when the God of Wisdom dwells in your heart, you will know the next step that you should take.

Read | Psalm 1:1–6

Reflect

1. Even though the book of Psalms is not considered part of the "wisdom literature" of the Bible, it nevertheless contains many insights into the wisdom of God.

According to the psalmist, what kind of person is considered "blessed"? What does that person do (see verses 1–2)?

2. As you discussed in this week's group time, the person who meditates on God's Word is "like a tree planted by streams of water" (verse 3). The imagery is one of stability. But what becomes of the person who does not heed God's wisdom (see verses 4–5)?

3. When is a specific time or moment in your life that God revealed his wisdom to you through His Word ? How did you act on this wisdom? What was the result?

4. The psalmist writes, "the LORD watches over the way of the righteous, but the way of the wicked leads to destruction" (verse 6). What hope does that give you today?

Pray | For your prayer time, do what the psalmist says: meditate on the Word of God, whether that's today's passage or another one. Let God's wisdom soak into you through his Word.

-Day 3-

Embodying Wisdom

The author of Hebrews wrote, "The Son is the radiance of God's glory and the exact representation of his being, sustaining all things by his powerful word. After he had provided purification for sins, he sat down at the right hand of the Majesty in heaven" (1:3). Jesus is the embodiment of God and all of God's characteristics—including wisdom. When you meditate on God's Word, you find that Jesus sets an excellent example of seeking wisdom, acting in wisdom, and growing in wisdom. Yes, even God incarnate had to *grow* in wisdom.

The Gospel of Luke tells us that when Jesus was twelve, he went with his earthly parents to celebrate the Passover in Jerusalem. We are not given all the details, but for some reason, when the Passover was over, Jesus' parents packed up and started the return to Nazareth without him. They had traveled for an entire day before they realized the oversight and went looking for him among their relatives and friends. But Jesus was nowhere to be found in their party.

So the panicked parents turned around and headed back to the city of Jerusalem. We again don't know how long they searched for Jesus when they arrived, but eventually they did locate him in the temple courts. And what was he doing there? "They found him in the temple courts, sitting among the teachers, listening to them and asking them questions" (Luke 2:46).

This provides us with great insights as to how Jesus sought wisdom. He went to the temple, listened to teachings on God's Word, and asked questions. (It's a pretty simple model to follow.) It is humbling to see Jesus—who knew the heart of God more intimately than any of us ever will—wanting to learn more about God's Word, listening to others teach on it, and then asking questions. We tend to think of Jesus as someone who didn't need to be taught, but even the Son of God studied the Word so he could know God better.

Read | Luke 2:46–52

Reflect

1. This passage in Luke relates what happened after Jesus' parents found him in the temple. What were the teachers' reactions to Christ (see verse 47)? What does this reveal about the way in which Jesus related to God and sought his wisdom?

2. If Jesus was God incarnate and at one with the Father, why do you think he still had questions about Scripture? What questions do you think he asked the teachers?

3. Jesus returned to Nazareth with his parents and "was obedient to them" (verse 51) —which was another act of humility. What happened as he did this (see verse 52)?

4. Jesus' approach was simple: go to a place of worship, listen to the teaching of God's Word, and ask questions. How do you model this approach in your life?

Pray | Take a few moments to reflect on the fact that even Jesus sought God's wisdom. Confess any times when you have taken shortcuts in your pursuit of his wisdom.

-Day 4-

Praying for Wisdom

Think again about the people and places that you typically go to for wisdom. Who are they? What are they? Maybe you often find wisdom in a trusted friend, a podcast, a book, or a teacher. These can be rich sources of wisdom. However, as previously noted, people whom we think are wise can fail us at times—and books, podcasts, and sermons won't give us all the guidance we need. What do we do in this situation? Simple. We go to the source.

The best way to acquire God's wisdom is to ask for it. King Solomon provides an excellent illustration of how this is done. In the time of his reign, kings in the near east were expected to be wise.[24] It fell on them to govern large populations of people, make decisions about war and trade, conduct relations with other nations—much like leaders do now. Only, it was common in those days for kings to give their gods the credit for their wisdom.[25] Solomon not only gave *God* credit for his wisdom, but he directly asked God for wisdom.

What is amazing about Solomon's story is that the Lord had appeared to him and said, "Ask for whatever you want me to give you" (1 Kings 3:5). If God appeared to you said you could have *anything*, what would you ask him to provide? If you're honest, it's probably not wisdom. We all tend to ask for whatever will serve our immediate needs: money, relationships, a job, health. But King Solomon actually asked for wisdom and a discerning heart.

Solomon was onto something. He knew that having wisdom would help him in all areas of his leadership and all areas of his life. For him, he truly believed that wisdom was a gift that was more precious than gold. He understood that wisdom is the gift that keeps on giving.

Read | 1 Kings 3:5–12

Reflect

1. The verses just before this passage reveal some of the reasons why Solomon needed wisdom. He had just made an alliance with Egypt, he was in the process of building

the temple in Jerusalem, and the people were still sacrificing "at the high places," where foreign gods were often worshiped. Why did Solomon want wisdom (see verse 9)?

2. The Lord was pleased that Solomon had asked for wisdom (see verse 10). How did he respond to Solomon? Why do you think he was so pleased with Solomon's request?

3. When you think about what you would request of God if he approached you in the same way that he approached Solomon, how could wisdom help you achieve what you want?

4. Where do you need wisdom in your leadership—whether you are leading at work, in your community, or at home? What would it look like to have a "discerning heart," like King Solomon requested, in your daily interactions with others?

Pray | End your time in prayer. Simply ask God for wisdom wherever and however you need it. Believe in the promises contained in his Word that he will give it to you.

— Day 5 —

A Lifelong Quest

You've likely heard the phrase, "Life is a marathon; not a sprint." Some of our greatest achievements will take years of intention, effort, and struggle in order for us to attain them. We won't gain them if we choose to focus on them for just a short while and then move on to something else. The same is true when it comes to wisdom. *It is a lifelong quest,* and we have to stay committed to pursuing it.

As you saw in yesterday's study, King Solomon asked God for wisdom, and the Lord graciously granted his request. In fact, the Bible tells us that "Solomon's wisdom was greater than the wisdom of all the people of the East, and greater than all the wisdom of Egypt" (1 Kings 4:30). But this doesn't mean that Solomon *remained* wise. Sadly, toward the end of his life, he began to be led astray. He married wives from nations that God had forbidden. He then started to worship other gods. He stopped seeking wisdom and sought worldly possessions instead (see 1 Kings 11:1–6).

Wisdom is not a sprint; it's a marathon. It's not a virtue we seek once; it's something we seek every day of our lives. In the words of one scholar, the quest for wisdom is *a long obedience in the same direction.*[26] Life changes, and we will face new challenges. For each obstacle we face, we need a fresh infusion of God's wisdom. We receive this wisdom by establishing a pattern of seeking it every day through the study of his Word.

When you became a Christian, your life was changed. But that was just the first step in the journey. Wisdom is the same way. You have to continually seek it all the days of your life, journeying with God as he gives you the wisdom you need for each season.

Read | Proverbs 3:1–8

Reflect

1. This passage represents another instance of a proverb being written in the form of a father giving instruction to his son. How would you describe the type of advice

that he is providing? What does the father say about continuing to seek wisdom (see verses 1–4)?

2. As you learned in this week's group time, there is an upper wisdom and a lower wisdom. Upper wisdom comes from God, while lower wisdom comes from our own understanding. What does the father say about this to his son (see verses 5–6)?

3. The father states that wisdom will bring "health to your body and nourishment to your bones" (verse 8). Why do you think this would be the case?

4. Who is the wisest person you know? How did that person become wise? What kind of wisdom do you want people to see in you when you are ninety years old?

Pray | Spend a few minutes reflecting on this week's personal study time. Did God convict you of anything this week? Did you change in any way? Or learn something new? Talk to God about what you learned this week and what he might be showing you today.

For Next Week

Before you meet again with your group next week, read pages 102–107 in chapter 7 of *The God of the Way*. Also go back and complete any of the study and reflection questions from this personal study that you weren't able to finish.

WEEK 5

BEFORE GROUP MEETING	Read pages 102–107 in chapter 7 of *The God of the Way* Read the Welcome section (page 105)
GROUP MEETING	Discuss the Connect questions Watch the video teaching for session 5 Discuss the questions that follow as a group Do the closing exercise and pray (pages 105–116)
PERSONAL STUDY – DAY 1	Complete the daily study (pages 118–119)
PERSONAL STUDY – DAY 2	Complete the daily study (pages 120–121)
PERSONAL STUDY – DAY 3	Complete the daily study (pages 122–123)
PERSONAL STUDY – DAY 4	Complete the daily study (pages 124–125)
PERSONAL STUDY – DAY 5 (before week 6 group meeting)	Complete the daily study (pages 126–127) Read chapter 8 in *The God of the Way* Complete any unfinished personal studies

God of Light

יהוה אורי

JEHOVAH ORI

[GOD IS MY LIGHT]

The LORD is my light and my salvation—
whom shall I fear?

PSALM 27:1

Welcome | Read On Your Own

In the last session, you explored the wisdom of God as revealed in the pages of his Word, the Bible. You saw that wisdom is something to be prized, cherished, and pursued as you grow in your relationship with Christ. Wisdom has the power to protect you from the world and transform you into the image of your Savior. While you won't receive all the wisdom you need all at once, the Lord will be faithful to provide it to you in your time of need as you are faithful to him.

God's light works in a similar way. The Lord won't always illuminate the *entire* journey for you. You won't always have perfect knowledge of every twist and turn in the road ahead. Rather, God will often light your way in increments, guiding you one step at a time as you learn to depend on him. "Your word is a lamp for my feet, a light on my path" (Psalm 119:105).

God is wisdom, and God is light. In a world filled with darkness, knowing that you have the God of light on your side should be incredibly comforting! Turn on the news, look at your phone, or pick up the paper, and it can seem that there is only darkness— death, war, struggles, pandemics, recessions. We all need God's divine light to cut through that darkness.

In this session, you will learn about that divine light as revealed in God's Word. You will see that God's Word is a powerful two-edged sword that cuts through the darkness surrounding us in this world. You will also explore what the Bible says about Jesus being the light of the world . . . and what that means for you today as a carrier of that light.

Connect | 15 minutes

Welcome to session 5 of *The God of His Word*. To get things started for this week's group time, discuss one of the following questions:

- What is a key insight or takeaway from last week's personal study that you would like to share with the group?

 — *or* —

- What are some ways that God has guided you in life step by step?

Watch | 20 minutes

Now watch the video for this session. As you watch, use the following outline to record any thoughts or concepts that stand out to you.

I. What are some of the ways that God lights our path?

   A. One of the ways that God reveals himself to us is through the light of his Word.

      1. The first thing God does in the creation story is command there to be light (see Genesis 1:3). What was that light? The sun, moon, and stars weren't created until the fourth day.

      2. The rabbis tell us this was not an ordinary light but was the supernatural light of God's presence. It was Jesus shining as a light in the midst of the darkness. But God saw the world would misuse the light, so he hid it for the righteous in the messianic kingdom.

   B. But God doesn't completely deny us access to the light. We can get a glimpse of some of that hidden light in the Word of God (see Proverbs 6:23). This is God's promise to us.

      1. God's Word is a lamp unto our feet and a light unto our path (see Psalm 119:105). Many times we are stumbling in the dark and need the light of God to reveal our situation.

Luminescent in God's Presence

"When Moses came down from Mount Sinai with the two tablets of the covenant law in his hands . . . his face was radiant because he had spoken with the LORD" (Exodus 34:29).

Light is critical to life on our planet, for almost all living things in this world depend on light for food and energy. Plants depend on light from the sun to produce their food through a process known as photosynthesis. Humans rely on light from the sun to provide vitamin D, maintain our internal body clocks, and live on a planet that is not too cold to sustain life. Without light, our eyes would be of no use. Our vision depends on the ability of our eyes to capture light and send images to our brain that we perceive as objects.[27] Light equals life.

But just as we can't survive *physically* without the light of the sun, so we can't survive *spiritually* without the light of the Son. If we do not have the light of God's presence, we cannot thrive or even survive in his kingdom. This is why life is found in the Word of God. The Bible is a vessel for God's truth and light! The more we study the Scriptures, the more the light from God breaks into our world and is revealed in our lives. We need this light from the Son.

When Moses ascended the slopes of Mount Sinai to receive the second set of the Ten Commandments—the Word of God—he was surrounded by God's light. He came down from the mountain literally ablaze with the radiance of God . . . a physical manifestation of the effects of being in the light of God's presence for forty days and forty nights. This is what happens when we spend time in God's Word. We become luminescent in his presence.

2. We also want God to light up the whole runway. We want to know the end from the beginning. But often God only shows the best steps that we should take in life one step at a time.

II. Why do some people prefer the darkness to the light?

A. There are several reasons why people may choose the misery of the darkness in this world over the peace and joy that God's light can bring.

1. Some people choose the darkness because they don't know anything else. They have endured such abuse and pain that the darkness is all that remains.

2. If we don't fill up our hearts with the light of God, we will fill it up with something else. We're going to fill it with addictions. We're going to fill it with unhealthy relationships. Space wasn't created to be empty. Space has to be filled with *something*.

3. The question for us spiritually is what we are allowing to fill that space in our hearts. God wants us to be whole, but we can't be made whole if we are holding on to unhealthy things. There always has to be *displacement* before there can be a *replacement*.

B. God's Word cuts like a knife (see Hebrews 4:12). It cuts away those things that are unhealthy within us.

1. We can be attached to people, substances, and all sorts of things. God's Word can cut away anything we are attached to that is not of God and that is not good for us.

2. There is a part of God's Word that is truth, but there is also a part of his Word that is grace. We can wield the sword of truth in such a way that we cut people to pieces. We have to look to the example of Christ to see how he handled God's Word.

III. What does Jesus reveal about the way we should handle God's light?

A. Jesus is the way, the truth, and the life (see John 14:6), but the first description of him is being "full of grace and truth" (John 1:14). Truth apart from grace is not life-giving.

1. Paul states that if we do not have love, we are just a "clanging cymbal" (1 Corinthians 13:1). Love is the greatest of all traits because it is the only thing that will last. Faith and hope won't exist in heaven . . . but what won't fade away is love.

2. "God is love" (1 John 4:8). We need the light *and* love that God reveals in his Word. Just as Jesus revealed light and love, we need to reveal his light and love in the same way.

B. The Word of God also reveals that we need to love ourselves. There is so much self-hatred today . . . but we need to see ourselves in the way that God sees us.

1. The Bible says that everything God made, he made good and beautiful. We are part of his creation. When we judge ourselves critically, we are actually judging the One who made us.

2. We need to ask what God's Word says about us and then speak those truths over ourselves until we believe them. God will illuminate the darkness of the lies we have been believing.

God's Word as a Two-Edged Sword

"The word of God is alive and active. Sharper than any double-edged sword, it penetrates even to dividing soul and spirit, joints and marrow; it judges the thoughts and attitudes of the heart. Nothing in creation is hidden from God's sight" (Hebrews 4:12–13).

The Word of God is like a double-edged sword in that it has two sides—truth *and* grace. When we wield the side that represents truth, we cut through the enemy's lies and any misperceptions we have of God. When we wield the side that represents grace, we learn about God's mercy toward us and the incredible lengths to which he went to be reconciled to us. God's Word, just like Jesus—the *living* Word—is "full of grace and truth" (John 1:14).

But there is another aspect of the Bible being a two-edged sword that is frequently overlooked. The counsel of Scripture has two sides to it: an *old* and a *new*. Many Christians settle for half an inheritance by only embracing the New Testament. On the other side, Jews have an incomplete picture when they only embrace the Old Testament. In reality, the Old Testament and the New fit together, and *both* are needed to experience the full picture of what God wants for our lives . . . and to fully understand Jesus as the Messiah.

Jesus once said, "Every teacher of the law who has become a disciple in the kingdom of heaven is like the owner of a house who brings out of his storeroom new treasures as well as old" (Matthew 13:52). The treasure of God's Word is found in both the Old and New Testaments. And *together*, their value increases dramatically.[28]

IV. How is God shining his light on us today?

    A. Jesus is the living Word and the light of the world (see John 8:12). We think of him as a carpenter, but the Greek word that describes his profession is *tektōn*—a craftsman. This is significant because he was present with God at the time of creation.

    B. Jesus is the *tektōn* or craftsman of creation. Just as God crafted the world, so Jesus came to craft our lives. He came to build the church, the community and family of God. He wants to take the rubble out of our lives and create something beautiful out of it.

    C. We are called to be God's shadow. A shadow exists because it comes off the reflection of the light. We were not meant to have an existence apart from God. We were created to be a reflection of his nature and an embodiment of the truth of God's Word in our lives.

Discuss | 35 minutes

Take some time to discuss what you just watched by answering the following questions. There are some suggested questions below to help you begin your discussion, but feel free to pick any of the additional questions as well as time allows.

Suggested Questions

1. In the story of creation, God commanded there to be light on the first day. However, the sun, moon, and stars are not created until the *fourth* day (see Genesis 1:3–5, 14–19). What is an explanation for the light that occurred on the first day of creation?

2. Read Proverbs 6:20–23. The father is instructing his son to not forsake God's commands but to "bind them always on [his] heart" (verse 21). According to these verses, how will these commands light his path? Why do you think God often doesn't show us the entire path all at once but only lights our way a few steps at a time?

3. Read John 8:12. When Jesus spoke these words, he was immediately challenged by the Pharisees because they recognized he was claiming to have been sent by God (see verses 13–16). What do you think Jesus meant by his statement that he is the "light" of the world? How has Christ brought his light into your life?

4. The disciple John wrote, "Light has come into the world, but people loved darkness instead of light because their deeds were evil" (John 3:19). What are some of the possible reasons as to why people often choose darkness over the light?

Additional Questions

5. The author of Hebrews says the Word of God is "sharper than any double-edged sword" (Hebrews 4:12). It illuminates our path like a lamp, guiding us in the way we should go, but it also sheds light on any darkness we are concealing in our hearts. What are some of ways that God's Word has served as a two-edged sword in your life?

6. John describes Jesus as coming into this world "full of grace and truth" (John 1:14). He brought God's truth to people, but he did it in a way that was full of grace. What does this say about how we should be approaching those in our lives who need God's truth? What is the danger in only using God's Word as an instrument that cuts?

7. Read 1 Corinthians 13:1–7. Paul mentions a number of gifts that people in the church can possess—gifts that instruct others and even serve their needs. However, what does he conclude about all these gifts if they are not administered in love? Why do you think Paul stresses this point of tempering our words and actions with grace?

8. In the story of creation, we read that God saw everything he had made and declared it "was very good" (Genesis 1:31). We are all part of God's creation, and thus included in this declaration . . . but often we don't see ourselves this way. What truth will you take away from this session to help you see yourself the way God sees you?

Respond | 10 minutes

Review the outline for the video teaching and any notes you took. In the space below, write down your most significant takeaway from this session.

Pray | 10 minutes

End your time by praying together as a group, asking the Lord to shine the light of his truth in your life and to help you present his truth to others in the way that Jesus did when he was on earth—with *grace*. Ask if anyone has any prayer requests to share. Write those requests down in the space below so you and your group members can pray about them in the week ahead.

Name   Request

Personal Study

As you discussed in your group time this week, our God is a God of light. This has two different implications. First, God lights our way and provides us with guidance in this life, much like carrying a lamp will illuminate a path that we are traveling. We won't always see the complete way forward, but we can trust that God will give us the light we need as we take each step. Second, God shines his light in a world filled with darkness. The Bible reveals that we have a spiritual enemy who is continually trying to fill our head with lies and cause us to doubt God's love and care for us. The light of God's Word exposes those falsehoods and causes the enemy to flee, much like a torch exposes what is in the darkness and causes the shadows to flee. Reflect on these truths as you study God's Word this week and what the Bible says about Jesus being the light of the world. Be sure to write down your responses to the questions in the spaces provided, as you will be given a few minutes to share your insights at the start of the next session if you are doing this study with others. If you are reading *The God of the Way* alongside this study, first review pages 102–107 in chapter 7 of the book.

-Day 1-

Our Darkest Moments

When you're a child, the dark is scary. You ask your parents to crack your bedroom door open, or leave the bathroom light on, or turn on a nightlight. You don't like the dark. As you grow older, your relationship with the dark changes. Maybe you're not afraid of it anymore. Maybe it's a place you like to go because you can hide there. Nobody can see what you're doing.

The dark can also be a place we unwillingly go. We find ourselves in a season of grief and everything around us feels dark. We go through times of intense anxiety. We go through times of doubt and times when we are unable to hear God's voice. Darkness, whether by choice or circumstance, overtakes us all at some point. But the good news is that darkness can never overcome light.

God's first act of creation was bestowing his light on the earth (see Genesis 1:3). The rabbis in Jewish tradition believed that this light—since it came before the creation of day and night on the fourth day—was the *shekinah*, the Hebrew word for the glory of God.[29] Tertullian, an early church father (c. AD 155–220) wrote, "God said, let there be light, and there was light. Immediately there appears the Word, that true light, which lights man on his coming into the world, and through Him also came light upon the world."[30]

Before God gave us anything else, he gave us his divine light to point us toward him. Even in our darkest moments, his light is there, available to us through his Word, the Spirit, and through Christ. The hope of *shekinah* can appear faint when we're in the darkness, but no matter how small the flame, it is there, shining the light into our dark places.

Read | Isaiah 60:19–20 and Ephesians 5:8–11

Reflect

1. Isaiah recorded the words of his prophecy for the Jewish exiles who were returning from captivity in foreign lands. These promises from God pointed to a great future

that God had in store for them. What does the prophet Isaiah say about the sun and moon? What does he say about God's light?

2. The apostle Paul wrote his words to the Ephesians to remind them that they were once spiritual exiles from God. How does he describe their before-and-after state?

3. What does Paul say is "the fruit of the light" (verse 9). How have you experienced the fruit of God's light during a dark time in your life?

4. Think about a dark area in your life, whether it is due to shame, grief, doubt, or something else. How would you like God's light to shine into that situation?

Pray | End your time in prayer. Ask God to bring his divine light to illuminate any dark places in your life. Don't be afraid of his light! It is kind and loving.

-Day 2-

A Lamp to My Feet

Many of us live in towns filled with bright lights—car headlights, street lights, lights on houses. Rarely do we experience true darkness, where electricity—or at least a battery-powered headlamp—is not available. It is only when we venture out into the countryside or places where no people live that we experience just how truly *dark* the darkness can be.

Of course, the people in Old Testament times didn't have electricity, streetlights, or headlamps. When they needed to light their homes, they lit an oil lamp. These were essentially small terracotta bowls filled with olive oil. A flax wick would be placed in the oil and lit on the end to illuminate a small area of a home. These lamps weren't powerful.[31] So, when the psalmist wrote, "Your word is a lamp to my feet and a light to my path" (Psalm 119:105 NKJV), this is what he meant. God's Word doesn't illuminate our entire future. It doesn't tell us what will happen next year or five years from now. It lights our path one step at a time.

We all want to know the full picture at all times. We want our path to be *fully* lit so we are never at a loss for what to do next and where to go next. But this is not how God works. He prefers to lead us one step at a time so that we learn to trust in him. He wants us to depend on him and his wisdom instead our own faulty understanding. This can be hard for us impatient types, but God's leading teaches us to let go of the control and rely on him. We don't have to know what will happen fifteen years from now. We just have to take one faithful step at a time.

Read | Psalm 119:105–112

Reflect

1. This passage is part of a longer psalm (in fact, the longest one that is in the Bible) in which the author reflects on the various benefits of obeying God's commands.

How does the psalmist feel about God's Word (which he also calls *laws, precepts, statutes,* and *decrees*)?

2. The psalmist admits that he is often afflicted and that life is not easy for him. What does he promise he will do when it comes to God's laws in spite of whatever trials he faces?

3. How has God's Word lit your path when you have likewise committed to obey God's commands? How did you receive that instruction? Was it something you read in the Bible, heard from a friend, gained from a sermon, or picked up somewhere else?

4. What next step do you need guidance for? How could God's Word help guide you?

Pray | Ask God to be a lamp unto your feet. Don't ask him to reveal your entire future. Instead, ask him to just help you trust in him for your next step.

—Day 3—

The Light of the World

The Feast of Tabernacles, which is also known as the Feast of Booths and *Sukkot*, is one of the seven feasts that the Lord commanded the Israelites to observe. It is also one of the three feasts the Jewish people were to observe where they had to "appear before the Lord your God at the place he will choose" (Deuteronomy 16:16).[32] This place was Jerusalem, and every year there was a great influx of pilgrims as they flooded into the city to celebrate the feast.

The Feast of Tabernacles was celebrated in the fall to commemorate the Exodus from Egypt (see Leviticus 23:33–43). It lasted for seven days, during which time the Israelites were to dwell in booths or tabernacles made from the branches of trees. (Hence the name.) During this feast, the people would light torches throughout the city, creating a beautiful display of light.[33] Jesus, like every other Jewish person, would have regularly attended this festival in Jerusalem.

It was on the final night of one of these festivals that Jesus told the crowd, "I am the light of the world. Whoever follows me will never walk in darkness, but will have the light of life" (John 8:12). As discussed during the group time, the Pharisees immediately challenged him on the statement. They cried out, "Here you are, appearing as your own witness; your testimony is not valid" (verse 13). They understood that Jesus was claiming to be the divine light of God.

God's Word is a lamp for our feet and light on our path, and Jesus—as *the* Word—is the embodiment of that light. This is a great promise in the midst of what feels like such a dark world. In the midst of pandemics, shootings, racial strife, and other tragedies, light can be hard to find. But Jesus' light is never smothered by the darkness. His light casts out the darkness with hope, love, understanding, compassion, and grace. The torches that lit up cities during the Feast of Tabernacles were bright . . . but Jesus' light shines brighter, and his light is forever.

Read | Matthew 5:13–16

Reflect

1. John wrote that Jesus is "the light of all mankind" (John 1:4). In this passage in Matthew, we see Jesus instructing his disciples to reflect his light to the world. What point is Jesus making about salt losing its saltiness and a light being hidden?

2. When Jesus states that "a town built on a hill cannot be hidden" (verse 14), he is referring to the fact that the people in the town will naturally fill their homes with lamps that provide light. What does this say about followers of Christ?

3. How and when did you first experience the light of Christ? What are some of the ways that you are seeking to "let your light shine before others" (verse 16)?

4. What feels especially dark in your city or community right now? Where do you sense Jesus in this darkness—if you sense his presence there at all?

Pray | Meditate on today's passage during your prayer time. Think about what it means that Jesus is the light of the world and that we are to carry his light. End your time by simply sitting in the light of Christ's presence, allowing it to fill you and provide you with peace.

— Day 4 —

Grace *and* Truth

In the personal study for session three, you spent some time identifying what your relationship with Scripture is like today. For some of you, this might have triggered painful memories. Perhaps God's Word has been used against you to accuse you or judge you. Perhaps someone abused the Word of God, hurting you with it rather than offering help and healing.

Sadly, this is a common experience for many Christians. God's Word *is* powerful, "sharper than any double-edged sword" (Hebrews 4:12). It exposes not only the lies of the enemy but also anything that is contrary to God's truth that we have allowed to dwell in our hearts. However, this does not mean that God's Word should be used as a weapon to wound others. Just as there is gun safety, there needs to be Word of God safety!

Jesus revealed that the two sides of the sword are truth *and* grace. Not one or the other—but both. John wrote, "The Word became flesh and made his dwelling among us. We have seen his glory, the glory of the one and only Son, who came from the Father, full of grace and truth" (John 1:14). Paul later added, "Let your conversation be always full of grace, seasoned with salt, so that you may know how to answer everyone" (Colossians 4:6).

Jesus told his followers, "You are the salt of the earth. But if the salt loses its saltiness, how can it be made salty again?" (Matthew 5:13). If our conversations are not "seasoned with salt," we won't be using God's Word in a way that yields grace and truth. Instead, we must look to the example of Christ—how he spoke with others and how he treated them. As we do, we will experience the healing that God's Word was intended to bring.

Read | John 4:6–26

Reflect

1. In this story, Jesus encountered a Samaritan woman who was drawing water from a well at noontime. This would have been the hottest part of the day, so it is likely

that this woman chose that time in order to avoid others. What truths did Jesus reveal about this woman?

2. How did Jesus show the Samaritan woman that he was there not only to show her the truth of her situation but also to show her grace? How did the woman respond?

3. The apostle Peter wrote, "Always be prepared to give an answer to everyone who asks you to give the reason for the hope that you have" (1 Peter 3:15). What does this say about the importance of knowing God's truth and being ready to share it?

4. Peter adds this caveat to his statement: "But do this with gentleness and respect" (1 Peter 3:15). What does this say about the importance of sharing God's grace?

Pray | End your time in prayer. If you need God's grace today, ask him to provide it to you. If you need his truth, ask him to provide that to you. Remember, they go hand in hand!

-Day 5-

No Darkness at All

Light is an interesting phenomenon. At its most basic level, scientists who study such things tell us that light is "electromagnetic radiation that can be detected by the human eye."[34] Think about what you see when you look at a rainbow. All the colors represent what your eye can pick up as light—from red to orange, yellow, green, blue, indigo, and finally violet. The color white comprises all the hues we can see on the light spectrum. The color black occurs when there is a complete absence of light. It can't exist in nature without any light at all.

Light is a metaphor that appears throughout Scripture. In Proverbs 4:18, we read that "the path of the righteous is like the morning sun, shining ever brighter till the full light of day." Paul describes those who follow God's ways as "[shining] like stars in the sky" (Philippians 2:15). Jesus used light in the Sermon on the Mount to describe what his followers should be doing: "Let your light shine before others, that they may see your good deeds" (Matthew 5:16). In that same sermon, Jesus told his followers that they were "the light of the world" (verse 14).

If light represents God and his goodness, then darkness represents evil and sin. When you look at the physical properties of light, such a comparison clearly makes sense. Darkness can only exist when light is not present. However, light can always dispel darkness. Just consider what happens when you walk into a dark room. You click on the light switch, and suddenly the room is illuminated and you can see everything. But the inverse is not true. The only way (on earth) to bring back the darkness is to turn off the light.

The disciple John wrote that "God is light; in him there is no darkness at all" (1 John 1:5). As we will see in this week's final study, that has certain implications for us as his followers.

Read | 1 John 1:5–10

Reflect

1. John states that he wrote this letter to proclaim what he witnessed personally during his time with "the Word of life" (verses 1). What was the message he received

from Christ? What does this mean for those who say they fellowship with God (see verses 5–6)?

2. There is no darkness at all in God, but this is unfortunately not the case for humans. What does John say about the darkness within us (see verses 8–9)?

3. John writes that if we "walk in the light, as he is in the light, we have fellowship with one another" (verse 7). How have you witnessed this in your community of faith? How does walking in the light of Christ create a bond between you and other believers?

4. Who is someone you know who shines bright with the love of Christ? How would you describe this person and the way you feel when you're around him or her?

Pray | Spend a few minutes reflecting on this week's personal study time. Did God convict you of anything this week? Did you change in any way? Or learn something new? Talk to God about what you learned this week and what he might be showing you today.

For Next Week

Before you meet again with your group next week, read chapter 8 in *The God of the Way*. Also go back and complete any of the study and reflection questions from this personal study that you weren't able to finish.

WEEK 6

BEFORE GROUP MEETING	Read chapter 8 in *The God of the Way* Read the Welcome section (page 131)
GROUP MEETING	Discuss the Connect questions Watch the video teaching for session 2 Discuss the questions that follow as a group Do the closing exercise and pray (pages 131–142)
PERSONAL STUDY – DAY 1	Complete the daily study (pages 144–145)
PERSONAL STUDY – DAY 2	Complete the daily study (pages 146–147)
PERSONAL STUDY – DAY 3	Complete the daily study (pages 148–149)
PERSONAL STUDY – DAY 4	Complete the daily study (pages 150–151)
PERSONAL STUDY – DAY 5	Complete the daily study (pages 152–153) Connect with your group about the next study that you want to go through together

God of All People

עמנו אל

IMMANUEL

[GOD WITH US]

*The virgin will conceive and give birth to a son,
and will call him Immanuel.*

ISAIAH 7:14

Welcome | Read On Your Own

In this study, you've learned about some of the different attributes of God as revealed in his Word. He is a creator. He is a lover of justice but also of mercy. He is all-powerful and wise. He shines the light of his truth to guide our way and expose the enemy's lies. Jesus is the embodiment of all of these traits of God. The Gospels are filled with stories of his power and wisdom, his justice for those who were oppressed, and his mercy for those who repented of their sins. He is "the light of the world" (John 8:12) . . . the *living* Word of God.

What's more, Jesus didn't reveal these attributes of God's character to just a select few. While he surrounded himself with a select group of disciples, instructing and empowering them to continue his mission after he left the earth, he interacted with people from all different backgrounds, economic conditions, and walks of life. When he chose to die on the cross as God's ultimate sacrifice, he paid the price for the sins of *everyone*. God's offer of salvation is available to *all* who choose to accept Jesus as their Savior.

Human beings are naturally drawn to clubs. We like to know who is "in" and who is "out." We form groups based on our theology, politics, and beliefs—typically at the exclusion of those who hold different opinions from our own. But God makes himself available to everyone. He even takes it one step further by extending an offer of adoption into his own family. The apostle Paul marveled at this truth when he wrote, "The Spirit you received brought about your adoption to sonship. And by him we cry, 'Abba, Father'" (Romans 8:15).

In this session, you will dig deeper into this reality that God loves *all* his children . . . even those who seem different from you. You will focus on one particular encounter that Jesus had with a woman and what that encounter means for us today. You will see that when you draw near to God, he will always draw near to you, no matter who you are.

Connect | 15 minutes

Welcome to session 6 of *The God of His Word*. To get things started for this week's group time, discuss one of the following questions:

- What is a key insight or takeaway from last week's personal study that you would like to share with the group?

— *or* —

• Have you ever been excluded from a club or an organization? Why were you excluded—and how did that make you feel?

Watch | 20 minutes

Now watch the video for this session. As you watch, use the following outline to record any thoughts or concepts that stand out to you.

I. What does the Bible reveal about who is included in God's mercy?

    A. The God of His Word doesn't exclude *anyone* from his grace, mercy, blessings, and promises.

        1. Jesus was always widening the circle and inviting people into God's family. We especially see this in the story of the woman with the flow of blood (see Mark 6:25–34).

        2. This woman had been in a state of *tumah* (ritual impurity) for *twelve years*. Under Jewish law, she was considered a *niddah*. Her husband could not have contact with her.

Laws Concerning the Unclean

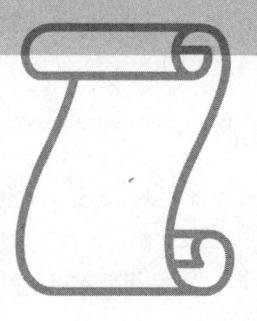

Under Jewish law, there were a number of conditions that could lead to a person being declared *tumah* or ritually unclean. Touching a dead body, or touching something that had been made impure by a corpse, made a person unclean for seven days (see Numbers 19:11, 16). Touching the carcass of a dead animal made a person unclean until evening (see Leviticus 11:24–25). A woman who gave birth was unclean for a period of time (see 12:2–5). Certain discharges and bleeding conditions would make a person unclean for as long as the condition lasted (see 15:1–33).[35] In the story of the bleeding woman, that lasted *twelve years*.

Other conditions could lead to a person being declared *tumah*. But perhaps the most feared was a condition that is typically translated in our Bibles as *leprosy*—though the disease actually refers to a number of disfigurative skin conditions. Those who were suspected of having the disease were required to go to a priest for examination. If found to be infected, they had to wear torn clothes, let their hair hang loose, cover their faces, cry out, "unclean, unclean," and live away from people for as long as the condition lasted (see Leviticus 13:2–3, 45–46).[36]

Leprosy was feared by the Israelites not only because of the damage done by the disease but also because of these strict isolation laws. Those with leprosy could find themselves ostracized from society for years—if not for a lifetime. This is why Jesus' healing of those with the condition is especially significant (see Luke 5:12–16; 17:11–19). Just as with the woman with the issue of blood, Christ not only healed them physically but also restored them relationally.[37]

B. For twelve years, this woman had received no physical touch or contact with people.

    1. She would have been emotionally feeling empty because of her state. She wouldn't have been able to go to the temple in Jerusalem, because no unclean person could enter. She was spiritually, physically, and relationally marginalized in society.

    2. The woman is so desperate that she goes to the village of Capernaum to see Jesus. She believes that if she can touch him, God will heal her. She has the faith to believe that something will happen.

II. What is the significance of the woman touching Jesus' garment?

    A. The woman reached out and touched the corner of his garment (the *kanaph*).

        1. The *kanaph* was a four-cornered garment worn by Jewish men. On the four corners were *tzitzit*, or ritual fringes. One of the things these *tzitzit* represent are the 613 commandments of God. When the Jewish people see these ritual fringes, they are reminded to keep God's commands.

2. The *tzitzit* also represent our priestly identity and calling. This woman was grabbing hold of God's promises and believing that she would be given a new identity. She couldn't even be touched by a family member, but here she was reaching out to a holy rabbi.

B. When we seek to encounter God, God always takes the first step toward us.

1. Jesus was on his way to do something else, but he felt the power leave his body. He asked, "Who touched my clothes?" (Mark 5:30). He already knew, but he did this for her and the people who were around, so that she would have to come forward.

2. Normally, when an unclean person touched a clean person, the clean person would become unclean. But there is so much healing in Jesus that she becomes clean and is healed. Jesus rose up with healing in his wings and transformed her in that moment (see Malachi 4:2).

III. What is the significance of this story for us today?

A. This is not just a story of the healing of a woman but has eternal value for us today.

1. There are four corners of the *kanaph*, which represent four aspects of exile that Adam and Eve received when they sinned: spiritual, relational, emotional, and physical exile.

2. God promises to redeem his people from the four corners of the earth (see Isaiah 11:12). Four is connected to *redemption* because God is undoing all these aspects of exile.

B. Jesus died on the cross to undo the physical, relational, spiritual, and emotional aspects of exile. The woman experienced healing and wholeness in these four areas because of her faith.

1. The woman showed faith in God and courage by reaching out to Jesus. She could have been even more banished if things didn't work out the way that she was hoping.

2. God loves it when we have a faith that is willing to express itself in taking risks. The woman took a great risk by reaching out to Jesus—and she was healed.

No Jew or Gentile

"So in Christ Jesus you are all children of God through faith, for all of you who were baptized into Christ have clothed yourselves with Christ. There is neither Jew nor Gentile, neither slave nor free, nor is there male and female, for you are all one in Christ Jesus" (Galatians 3:26–28).

When we read these words, we might assume that Paul is saying there should be no distinctions *at all* between people in God's family. But this interpretation is difficult to reconcile with John's vision in the book of Revelation, where he describes seeing "a great multitude that no one could count, from every nation, tribe, people and language, standing before the throne and before the Lamb" (7:9). In fact, such passages reveal that God *loves* the diversity of ethnicities and nations—and men and women—because they each express a different aspect of his nature. It's much like a multi-faceted diamond. What makes the diamond sparkle and shine brilliantly are all the different facets that absorb and reflect the light.

What Paul is actually stating in this passage is that in God's estimation, there is complete *spiritual* equality among his people. This was an important point for Paul to stress in the days of the early church. The believers who came from Jewish and Gentile backgrounds were often at odds with one another, with each group claiming some superiority over the other. Paul's message to those who would seek to elevate themselves in this manner is that there are no second-class citizens in God's kingdom. Instead, all are one in God's sight.

IV. What other truths can we learn about the God of all people from this story?

A. This story reveals something signficant about how Jesus interacted with women. In ancient culture—both Jewish and Greco-Roman—women were generally not valued.

    1. In Greco-Roman culture, women were considered property. Women were more valued in Jewish culture, but the understanding held by the rabbis (based on passages such as Psalm 45:13) was that the "glory" or domain of the woman was in the home.

    2. Women were not to be involved in the affairs of the community or play a significant role in the spiritual life of God's people. Women could be involved in the synagogue, but they never held a leadership role, and first-century rabbis did not have women disciples.

B. The most radical feminist the world has ever known is Jesus! He valued women in a way that they had never been valued before, which is likely why they followed him in droves.

    1. Women (both wealthy and poor) supported Jesus' ministry, cleaned for him, ministered to him, fed him, and loved him. They sat at his feet and learned from him, just like the men.

    2. Women were Jesus' disciples and played a key role in the spread of the gospel. Some of the apostles' daughters, like Philip's, were prophets (see Acts 21:8–9). There were women teachers, like Priscilla (see Acts 18:26), and women apostles (see Romans 16:7).

C. Women held roles in the highest spiritual positions in the early church. But over time, this got lost as the church began to be more male-dominated and a hierarchy was established.

    1. We need to make sure women are empowered. We need to remember that God is the God of all people and that women played a key role in the formation of the early church.

    2. We are children of the God of all people. Whoever receives Christ has the right to be called a child of God. Racism, discrimination, and sexism simply cannot be allowed to exist among God's people.

Discuss | 35 minutes

Take some time to discuss what you just watched by answering the following questions. There are some suggested questions below to help you begin your discussion, but feel free to pick any of the additional questions as well as time allows.

Suggested Questions

1. The disciple John wrote, "For God so loved the world that he gave his one and only Son, that whoever believes in him shall not perish but have eternal life" (John 3:16). What do you think John means in this verse when he states that God loves "the world"?

2. Read Luke 8:43–48 and Leviticus 15:19–27. The bleeding woman had been unclean for twelve years. What do you think her life had been like during those years? Why do you think she was desperate enough to defy Jewish law by approaching Jesus?

3. Jesus told the woman, "Daughter, your faith has healed you" (Luke 8:48). She is the only person in the New Testament to be called *daughter* by Christ. What is the significance of Jesus using this term for her? What was he saying about her status before God?

4. Who might be considered the "unclean" in your community—those who are often left out, marginalized, or ostracized? What would Jesus do for those people to make them feel included? How might Jesus be calling *you* to partner with him in that work?

Additional Questions

5. The bleeding woman touched Jesus' *tzitzit*—the tassels on the corners of his garment (see Numbers 15:37–41). For the Jewish people, these tassels represented the four types of exile experienced after the Fall: spiritual, relational, emotional, and physical. What was the significance of the woman touching this part of Jesus' garment?

6. Jesus said, "I am the way and the truth and the life. No one comes to the Father except through me" (John 14:6). Some people claim this is too restrictive—that it *excludes* people from God's kingdom. But what is Jesus actually saying here? What is the invitation that he is extending—and to whom is he extending it?

7. The church should look like a preview of heaven—a place where all belong and feel loved by God. Think about your community of faith. Does it look like a preview of heaven? What can you do today to make it more inclusive for all believers in Christ?

Respond | 10 minutes

Review the outline for the video teaching and any notes you took. In the space below, write down your most significant takeaway from this session.

Pray | 10 minutes

End your time by praying together as a group, expressing your praise to God for including you in his plan of salvation. Ask if anyone has any prayer requests to share. Write those requests down in the space below so you and your group members can pray about them in the week ahead.

Name   Request

Personal Study

As you discussed in your group time this week, our God is a God of all people. When the woman whom Jewish society deemed to be unclean reached out to Jesus and touched his cloak, the Lord didn't rebuke her or tell her that she had done something inappropriate. Instead, he called her *daughter* and said her faith in him had brought her healing. Jesus told her to go in peace and to be freed from her suffering—revealing that "God does not show favoritism but accepts from every nation the one who fears him and does what is right" (Acts 10:34–35). In God's eyes, all are on an equal spiritual footing when it comes to acceptance in his kingdom. Reflect on these truths as you study God's Word this week. Be sure to write down your responses in the spaces provided and, if you are doing this study with others, consider reaching out to at least one person in your group to share your thoughts and insights. If you are reading *The God of the Way* alongside this study, first review pages 102–107 in chapter 7 of the book.

-Day 1-

Accepted Physically

The Hebrew law was written as a guide for the Israelites. It informed them not only on how God expected them to live and act, but also provided a way for them to keep order and keep safe. A part of the law dictated what was safe to eat (clean) and what was considered unsafe (unclean). It also dictated who was safe to be around and who wasn't based on their cleanliness.

A woman who was menstruating was considered ritually unclean or impure. Because of this, if a woman was bleeding, she could not have any physical contact with friends or family. She also had to remain isolated from her community until the bleeding stopped.[38] The Old Testament law stated, "Any bed she lies on while her discharge continues will be unclean . . . anything she sits on will be unclean . . . anyone who touches them will be unclean" (Leviticus 15:26–27).

The woman with the issue of blood in the Gospels had been bleeding for *twelve years*. Not only was she ritually unclean, but she had been in that state of uncleanliness for more than a decade. You can imagine how her community had grown weary of her. You can imagine that she felt deep shame over having a sickness that deemed her impure.

Our laws might not declare those who are sick to be unclean, but our society often treats them that way. What Jesus reveals in the story of the bleeding woman is that he accepts our bodies as they are. He did not reject the woman who reached out to him. He did not shame her for breaking the law and touching him. He simply accepted her presence, spoke to her, and made her well.

Read | Mark 5:25–34

Reflect

1. Jesus was on his way to the home of Jairus, one of the synagogue leaders, to heal his daughter (see verses 22–24). But when the woman with the issue of blood touched

his cloak, he felt the power flow out of him and stopped to see who had touched him (see verse 30). How does Mark describe the woman's condition (see verses 26–29)?

2. The disciples stated the obvious when Jesus asked who had touched his cloak: "You see the people crowding against you . . . and yet you can ask, 'Who touched me?'" (verse 31). What happened when the woman approached Jesus and told him what she had done? What does Jesus' reaction reveal about how he felt about her (see verses 33–34)?

3. When have you felt unaccepted because of your body—whether that was due to illness or the way your body looks? What does this story reveal about the way God sees you?

4. Do you find it difficult to believe that you are a part of God's good and beautiful creation—and that his creation includes *you*? Explain your response.

Pray | During your prayer time today, be honest with God about how you feel about your body and how you talk about your body. Ask him to help you know your body is good. No matter how you look or feel, you are his daughter or son.

-Day 2-
Accepted Socially

In the story of the woman with the issue of blood, we see Jesus accepting someone who was considered by Jewish law to be *unclean*. But we also see him accepting someone who was not empowered in the culture of the day: a *woman*. In Greco-Roman culture, women were not regarded as equal to men under the law. They received only a basic education and were always under the authority of a man (first her father and then her husband).[39]

Women were more valued in Jewish culture, but even then, they were considered most valuable in the home. They were not to go often out into public places or the main streets.[40] However, the bleeding woman was out in public, on a busy street in Capernaum, and—even more shocking—had touched Jesus' garment. Touching a man in public, even if he were the woman's husband, was (and is) considered immodest by Jewish law.[41]

The woman violated all these social rules, yet Jesus did not chastise her. Instead, he acknowledged her. From Jesus, we learn that social barriers that hold people back and keep them silent will not be tolerated. He blew right through them all—and not just with this woman, but with other women in Scripture as well (see Luke 13:10–12; John 4:27; 8:10–11).

You don't have to be a woman to understand what it feels like to be ostracized. Our culture elevates certain groups of people over others, deciding who is in and who is out. This is not the way of Christ. In him, outcasts are elevated and the silent are given a voice.

Read | Romans 16:1–4 and Acts 18:24–26

Reflect

1. In the passage from Romans, the apostle Paul indicates that Phoebe is a *deacon*. The term refers to a follower of Christ who was designated to serve with the elders of the church. What does Paul ask the congregation for her on his behalf?

2. How does Paul refer to Priscilla? What does he say that she and her husband, Aquila, did for him? What does this tell you about the roles women had in the early church?

3. What does the passage in the book of Acts reveal about the role that Pricilla had in the early church?

4. Have you ever been limited by a person or organization based on your gender, race, or social class? If so, what was that experience (or experiences) like for you?

Pray | Think about how you reacted to today's study. Perhaps you feel anger toward those who have tried to silence you in the past. Or maybe you feel guilty about taking part in silencing others. However you are feeling, bring those emotions to the Lord. Ask him for what you need.

Day 3

Moving Past Fear

Suffering is disheartening. It can beat us down, especially when our suffering is ongoing and lasts for a season. We can easily succumb to it and believe that this is our fate in life—that the healing won't come, the restoration is unreachable, the miracle is impossible.

But this isn't what we see in the story of the woman with the issue of blood. The Bible tells us that she had been suffering for twelve years. If that wasn't bad enough, we also read that "she had suffered a great deal under the care of many doctors and had spent all she had, yet instead of getting better she grew worse" (Mark 5:26). But instead of feeling resigned to her situation, she was proactive in her suffering. Since the doctors had failed her, she went to the source—straight to the man she had heard about who was ministering in Galilee.

This is what Jesus calls us to do. We are to *come to him* when we are weary, suffering, afraid, or uncertain. Instead of being paralyzed by fear and anxiety, we are to come to Christ. This is what the woman did. "She came up behind him in the crowd and touched his cloak" (verse 27). She knew that she was unclean and that it was not her place to touch his cloak. She didn't know how Jesus would respond when she touched him. But she didn't let her fears stop her, because she did know one thing: "If I just touch his clothes, I will be healed" (verse 28).

We don't have to sneak up on Jesus. We know how he will receive us—with open arms! And we don't have to question what will happen. When we come to him, we will be healed.

Read | Matthew 7:7–8; Matthew 11:28–30; and Hebrews 4:14–16

Reflect

1. Take a moment to review each of the promises that are made in these passages. According to these verses, how do we receive rest, blessings, mercy, and grace?

2. Are there any conditions put on us in order for us to receive these gifts? What does this tell you about the way in which we can approach "God's throne of grace"?

3. When was the last time you approached God's throne of grace and came to him with a request? What did you ask for? What happened as a result?

4. How do you typically approach God with your requests? Do you approach him with confidence . . . or with trepidation? What promises are you given in each of these passages (and the story of the bleeding woman) that God will hear your requests?

Pray | Come before the Lord. You don't have to be cleaned up. You don't have to have things sorted out. Just come as you are. Sit before him. Tell him what you need—whether it's healing, grace, forgiveness, or something else. Believe that he is capable of giving it to you.

-Day 4-

Salvation for All

The story of the bleeding woman is often described as an account of a miraculous healing. But as you've been learning this week, the story is also about acceptance. Jesus *accepted* the woman even though she was considered ritually unclean. He *accepted* the woman even though his culture said he should do the opposite. He accepted her—just as God accepts *all* people.

We know the woman touched the hem of Jesus' garment and was healed, but she wasn't simply touching his cloak. She was touching the *ritual tassels* of his cloak, known in Hebrew as the *tzitzit*—a tradition based on Mosaic law: "You are to make tassels on the corners of your garments, with a blue cord on each tassel. You will have these tassels to look at and so you will remember all the commands of the LORD" (Numbers 15:38–39).[42]

These tassels are also mentioned in a prophecy found later in the Old Testament: "'And many peoples and powerful nations will come to Jerusalem to seek the LORD Almighty and to entreat him.' This is what the LORD Almighty says: 'In those days ten people from all languages and nations will take firm hold of one Jew by the hem of his robe and say, "Let us go with you, because we have heard that God is with you"'" (Zechariah 8:22–23).

The message is this: all people are welcome to touch the hem of Christ's garment! We are all invited to accept Jesus' offer of salvation and become a part of God's family. It was a scandalous notion back in Jesus' day . . . and it remains one still today. But this is God's church—the one Jesus came to build—and he accepts all who come to him.

Read | Acts 10:1–48

Reflect

1. This story reveals a gulf that existed in the early church between the believers who came from a Jewish background and those who came from a Gentile background.

In this case, Cornelius was not just a Gentile but also a centurion in the Roman army. But what do we learn about Cornelius' relationship with God (see verses 1–6)?

2. Peter was shocked when God told him to "kill and eat" (verse 13) because the animals he saw were prohibited for food according to Jewish law (see Leviticus 11:41–43; Deuteronomy 14:7–19). What point was God making by asking Peter to eat these animals? What did Peter later reveal that he had learned (see Acts 10:28)?

3. What is the lesson for us today when it comes to not calling "anything impure that God has made clean" (verse 15)?

4. Do you have any fears that God does not accept you—either because of what you have done in the past or because of some other reason? What reassurance does this story provide to you?

Pray | End your time in prayer. Ask God to help you see yourself and others through his eyes: as his children who are worthy of his salvation through grace.

– Day 5 –
A Welcoming Community

The Gospels reveal that Jesus not only broke social norms by speaking to women in public but also broke social norms by associating with Romans (see Luke 7:1–10), tax collectors (see Luke 19:1–10), and a wide array of "sinners" (see Luke 5:27–32). His actions shocked the religious elite. Jesus sought salvation not just for the Jews but also for the Gentiles. He crossed social boundaries, touched the unclean, and taught grace above the law.

Why did he do this? So we would do this as well. As Christ followers, we are to walk in his footsteps—and Jesus' footsteps took him to the shady parts of town, on the other side of the tracks, and into homes of people who had . . . reputations. And then he said: *follow me*.

How can the church follow Jesus? Think about your own church community. Is it a group of people who look like you, talk like you, and have the same social or financial standing as you? Is the parking lot full of the same types of cars? Do your kids go to the same types of schools? Is this what Jesus intended for his church—for us to gather in groups based on sameness?

It's no wonder the church is often a turn-off for people. We are not always the most welcoming bunch or the most diverse. But if the church is to follow Jesus, shouldn't we work to make it a safe place for the outcast, the sick, and the "unclean"? Shouldn't it naturally be full of people who haven't been able to fit in or find a home elsewhere? Because in Christ, we are all—Jew and Gentile, male and female—children of God. In Christ, we are a family.

Read | Luke 7:36–47

Reflect

1. Notice how Luke sets the scene for this story. Jesus had been invited to dine in the home of a man named Simon, who was a Pharisee. While Jesus was there, a woman "who lived a sinful life" (verse 37) entered uninvited and began to wash Jesus' feet with her tears. What do you think motivated this woman to take this bold action?

2. When Simon witnessed this taking place, he said to himself, "If this man were a prophet, he would know who is touching him" (verse 39). Jesus knew his thoughts. How did he reply to Simon? What did Jesus' parable reveal about Simon's heart (see verses 40–43)?

3. How did Jesus say this woman had treated him better than Simon had treated him?

4. How do you relate to the woman in this story? How has Jesus' forgiveness affected you personally? How has it affected the way you view and treat others?

Pray | Spend a few minutes reflecting on this week's personal study time. Did God convict you of anything this week? Did you change in any way? Or learn something new? Talk to God about what you learned this week and what he might be showing you today.

Leader's Guide

Thank you for your willingness to lead your group through this study! What you have chosen to do is valuable and will make a great difference in the lives of others. *The God of His Word* is a six-session Bible study built around video content and small-group interaction. As the group leader, imagine yourself as the host of a party. Your job is to take care of your guests by managing the details so that when your guests arrive, they can focus on one another and on the interaction around the topic for that session.

Your role as the group leader is not to answer all the questions or reteach the content—the video, book, and study guide will do most of that work. Your job is to guide the experience and cultivate your small group into a connected and engaged community. This will make it a place for members to process, question, and reflect—not necessarily receive more instruction.

There are several elements in this leader's guide that will help you as you structure your study and reflection time, so be sure to follow along and take advantage of each one.

Before You Begin

Before your first meeting, make sure the group members have a copy of this study guide. Alternately, you can hand out the study guides at your first meeting and give the members some time to look over the material and ask any preliminary questions. Also make sure they are aware that they have access to the streaming videos at any time by following the instructions printed on the inside front cover. During your first meeting, ask the members to provide their name, phone number, and email address so you can keep in touch with them.

Generally, the ideal size for a group is eight to ten people, which will ensure that everyone has enough time to participate in discussions. If you have more people, you might want to break up the main group into smaller subgroups. Encourage those who show up at the first meeting to commit to attending for the duration of the study, as this will help the group members get to know one another, create stability for the group, and help you know how to best prepare to lead them through the material.

Each of the sessions begins with an opening reflection in the "Welcome" section. The questions that follow in the "Connect" section serve as an icebreaker to get the group members thinking about the topic. Some people may want to tell a long story in response to one of these questions, but the goal is to keep the answers brief. Ideally, you want everyone in the group to get a chance to answer, so try to keep the responses to a minute or less. If you have talkative group members, say up front that everyone needs to limit their answer to one minute.

Give the group members a chance to answer, but also tell them to feel free to pass if they wish. With the rest of the study, it's generally not a good idea to have everyone answer every question—a free-flowing discussion is more desirable. But with the opening icebreaker questions, you can go around the circle. Encourage shy people to share, but don't force them.

At your first meeting, let the group members know each session contains a personal study section they can use to continue to engage with the content until the next meeting. While this is optional, it will help them cement the concepts presented during the group study time and help them better understand the character, nature, and attributes of the God of His Word. Let them know that if they choose to do so, they can watch the video for the next session by accessing the streaming code found on the inside front cover of their studies. Invite them to bring any questions and insights to your next meeting, especially if they had a breakthrough moment or didn't understand something.

Preparation for Each Session

As the leader, there are a few things you should do to prepare for each meeting:

- **Read through the session.** This will help you become more familiar with the content and know how to structure the discussion times.

- **Decide how the videos will be used.** Determine whether you want the members to watch the videos ahead of time (again, via the streaming access code found on the inside front cover) or together as a group.

- **Decide which questions you want to discuss.** Based on the length of your group discussions, you may not be able to get through all the questions. So look over the recommendations for the suggested and additional questions in each session and choose which ones you definitely want to cover.

- **Be familiar with the questions you want to discuss.** When the group meets, you'll be watching the clock, so make sure you are familiar with the questions that you have selected. In this way, you will ensure that you have the material more deeply in your mind than your group members.

- **Pray for your group.** Pray for your group members and ask God to lead them as they study his Word.

In many cases, there will be no one "right" answer to the question. Answers will vary, especially when the group members are being asked to share their personal experiences.

Structuring the Discussion Time

You will need to determine with your group how long you want to meet so you can plan your time accordingly. Suggested times for each section have been provided in this study guide, and if you adhere to these times, your group will meet for ninety minutes, as noted below. If you want to meet for two hours, follow the times given in the right-hand column:

Section	90 Minutes	120 Minutes
CONNECT (discuss one or more of the opening questions for the session)	15 minutes	20 minutes
WATCH (watch the teaching material together and take notes)	20 minutes	20 minutes
DISCUSS (discuss the study questions you selected ahead of time)	35 minutes	50 minutes
RESPOND (write down key takeaways)	10 minutes	15 minutes
PRAY (pray together and dismiss)	10 minutes	15 minutes

As the group leader, it is up to you to keep track of the time and keep things on schedule. You might want to set a timer for each segment so both you and the group members know when your time is up. Don't be concerned if the group members are quiet or slow to share. People are often quiet when they are pulling together their ideas, and this might be a new experience for them. Just ask a question and let it hang in the air until someone shares. You can then say, "Thank you. What about others? What came to you when you watched that portion of the teaching?"

Group Dynamics

Leading a group through *The God of His Word* will prove to be highly rewarding both to you and your group members. But you still may encounter challenges along the way! Discussions can get off track. Group members may not be sensitive to the needs and ideas of others. Some might worry they will be expected to talk about matters that make them feel awkward. Others may express comments that result in disagreements. To help ease this strain on you and the group, consider the following ground rules:

- When someone raises a question or comment that is off the main topic, suggest that you deal with it another time, or, if you feel led to go in that direction, let the group know you will be spending some time discussing it.

- If someone asks a question that you don't know how to answer, admit it and move on. At your discretion, feel free to invite group members to comment on questions that call for personal experience.

- If you find one or two people are dominating the discussion time, direct a few questions to others in the group. Outside the main group time, ask the more dominating members to help you draw out the quieter ones. Work to make them a part of the solution instead of part of the problem.

- When a disagreement occurs, encourage the group members to process the matter in love. Encourage those on opposite sides to restate what they heard the other side say about the matter, and then invite each side to evaluate if that perception is accurate. Lead the group in examining other Scriptures related to the topic and look for common ground.

When any of these issues arise, encourage your group members to follow these words from Scripture: "Love one another" (John 13:34); "If it is possible, as far as it depends on you, live at peace with everyone" (Romans 12:18); and, "Be quick to listen, slow to speak and slow to become angry" (James 1:19). This will make your group time more rewarding and beneficial for everyone who attends.

Thank you again for taking the time to lead your group. You are making a difference in your group members' lives and having an impact on their journey toward a better understanding of the God of His Word.

Endnotes

1. Joseph Shulam, "Rabbis and Their Disciples Between the 1st Century BC and the 2nd Century AD," Renew.org, https://renew.org/rabbis-and-their-disciples-between-the-1st-century-b-c-and-the-2nd-century-a-d/.
2. Mike Leake, "What Does Elohim Mean and Why Is This Name of God so Important?" Bible Study Tools, https://www.biblestudytools.com/bible-study/topical-studies/elohim-supreme-one-mighty-one.html.
3. Kathie Lee Gifford and Rabbi Jason Sobel, *The God of the Way* (Nashville, TN: Thomas Nelson), 85.
4. Charles Spurgeon, "Magnificat," sermon #340, delivered October 14, 1860.
5. Kendra Cherry, "What a Messy Room Says About You," Very Well Mind, August 2, 2021, https://www.verywellmind.com/psychology-of-a-messy-room-4171244#toc-disadvantages-of-messiness.
6. Gifford and Sobel, *The God of the Way*, 92.
7. "Hebrew Names of God: 'El'—Might, Strength, Power," Hebrew4Chrisians, https://www.hebrew4christians.com/Names_of_G-d/El/el.html.
8. Leake, "What Does Elohim Mean and Why Is This Name of God so Important?" https://www.biblestudytools.com/bible-study/topical-studies/elohim-supreme-one-mighty-one.html.
9. Gifford and Sobel, *The God of the Way*, 52.
10. "What Is the Meaning of Yahweh? What Is the Meaning of *Jehovah*?" GotQuestions.org, https://www.gotquestions.org/meaning-of-Yahweh.html; "Names of God in Judaism," Wikipedia, https://www.cs.mcgill.ca/~rwest/wikispeedia/wpcd/wp/n/Names_of_God_in_Judaism.htm#:~:text=Jews%20also%20call%20God%20Adonai,of%20the%20Greek%20name%20Adonis.
11. Gifford and Sobel, *The God of the Way*, 86–87.
12. "Jehovah," Bible Study Tools, https://www.biblestudytools.com/dictionary/jehovah/.
13. Gifford and Sobel, *The God of the Way*, 90.
14. Rabbi Jason Sobel, *Mysteries of the Messiah* (Nashville, TN: W Publishing, 2021), xiii.
15. "Jewish Concepts: Honey," Jewish Virtual Library, https://www.jewishvirtuallibrary.org/honey.
16. Gary Alley, "Israel's Seven Species: Honey," Jerusalem Cornerstone Foundation, https://www.jerusalemcornerstone.org/news/2014/09/14/israels-seven-species-honey.
17. Walter W. Wessel and Mark L. Strauss, *The Expositor's Bible Commentary: Mark* (Grand Rapids, MI: Zondervan, 2010), 704.
18. Alan F. Johnson, *The Expositor's Bible Commentary: Revelation* (Grand Rapids, MI: Zondervan, 2006), 678.
19. Ziony Zevit, "Invoking Creation in the Story of the Ten Plagues," TheTorah.com, https://www.thetorah.com/article/invoking-creation-in-the-story-of-the-ten-plagues.
20. "Logos," Britannica, https://www.britannica.com/topic/logos.
21. "How Is Jesus 'the Word'?" Verse by Verse Ministry, July 23, 2010, https://versebyverseministry.org/bible-answers/how-is-jesus-the-word.
22. "Dead Sea Researchers Discover Freshwater Springs and Numerous Micro-Organisms," Science Daily, September 27, 2011, https://www.sciencedaily.com/releases/2011/09/110927112546.htm.
23. Sobel, *Mysteries of the Messiah*, 20.
24. John H. Walton, Victor H. Matthews, and Mark W. Chavalas, *The IVP Bible Background Commentary: Old Testament* (Downers Grove, IL: IVP Academic), 421.
25. Walton, Matthews, and Chavalas, *The IVP Bible Background Commentary*, 421.
26. Eugene Peterson, *A Long Obedience in the Same Direction: Discipleship in an Instant Society* (Downers Grove, IL: InterVarsity Press, 2000).
27. Briana Lipor, "The Uses of Light," The Visible Spectrum, April 1, 2020, https://www.reflective-concepts.com/en-us/blog/the-uses-of-light#:~:text=Almost%20all%20living%20beings%20depend,by%20the%20process%20of%20photosynthesis.
28. Sobel, *Mysteries of the Messiah*, ix–x.
29. Troy Lacey and Bodie Hodge, "Light Before the Sun," Answers in Genesis, August 10, 2019, https://answersingenesis.org/days-of-creation/days-without-sun-what-was-source-light/.
30. Tertullian, *Against Praxeas*, chapter 12, http://www.newadvent.org/fathers/0317.htm.

31. Gary Byers, "The Lesson of the Lamp," Associates for Biblical Research, August 26, 2014, https://biblearchaeology.org/research/devotionals/4131-the-lesson-of-the-lamp.

32. "What Is the Feast of Tabernacles/Booths/Sukkot?" Got Questions, https://www.gotquestions.org/Feast-of-Tabernacles.html.

33. Craig S. Keener, *The IVP Bible Background Commentary: New Testament* (Dower's Grove, Illinois: InterVarsity Press, 1993), 285.

34. "Early Particle and Wave Theories," Britannica, https://www.britannica.com/science/light/Early-particle-and-wave-theories.

35. "Tumah and Taharah," Wikipedia, https://en.wikipedia.org/wiki/Tumah_and_taharah#:~:text=In%20Jewish%20law%2C%20%E1%B9%ADumah%20(Hebrew,a%20state%20of%20ritual%20impurity.

36. "Why Is Leprosy Talked About so Much in the Bible?," Got Questions, https://www.gotquestions.org/Bible-leprosy.html.

37. J.I. Packer, Merrill C. Tenney, and William White Jr., *Daily Life in Bible Times* (Nashville, TN: Thomas Nelson, 1982), 100–102.

38. Gifford and Sobel, *The God of the Way*, 112.

39. "The Roman Empire in the First Century: Women," PBS, https://www.pbs.org/empires/romans/empire/women.html.

40. Tehillim Psalms (Brooklyn, NY: Artscroll Mesorah, 2005), 572.

41. Gifford and Sobel, *The Rock, the Road, and the Rabbi* (Nashville, TN: Thomas Nelson, 2018), 85–86.

42. Gifford and Sobel, *The Rock, the Road, and the Rabbi*, 86

ALSO AVAILABLE

The God the Way
ISBN 9780785290438
On sale September 2022

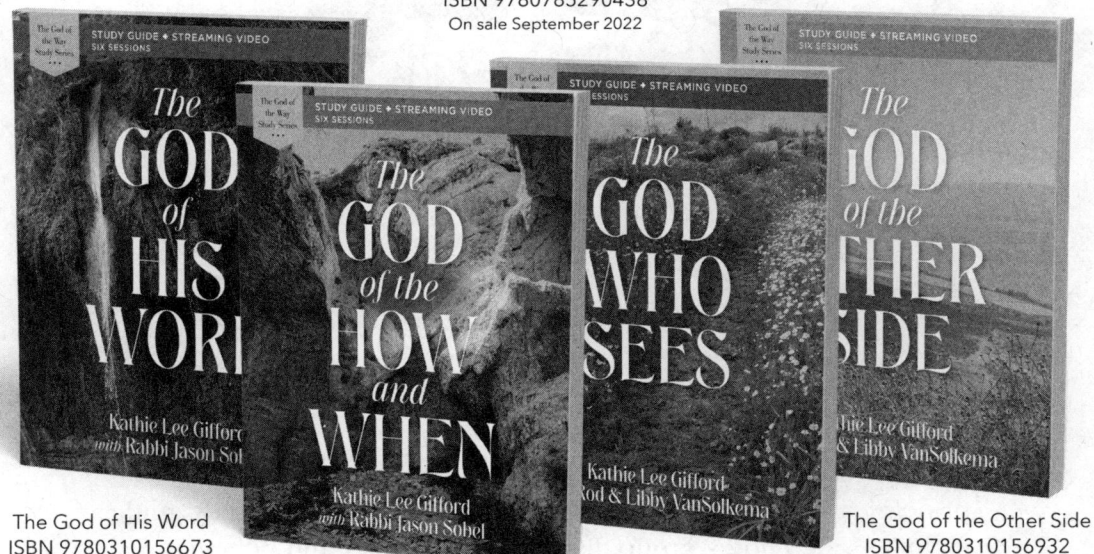

The God of His Word
ISBN 9780310156673
On sale April 2023

The God of the How and When
ISBN 9780310156543
On sale November 2022

The God Who Sees
ISBN 9780310156802
On sale July 2023

The God of the Other Side
ISBN 9780310156932
On sale January 2024

Available wherever books are sold

W Publishing Group

Harper Christian Resources

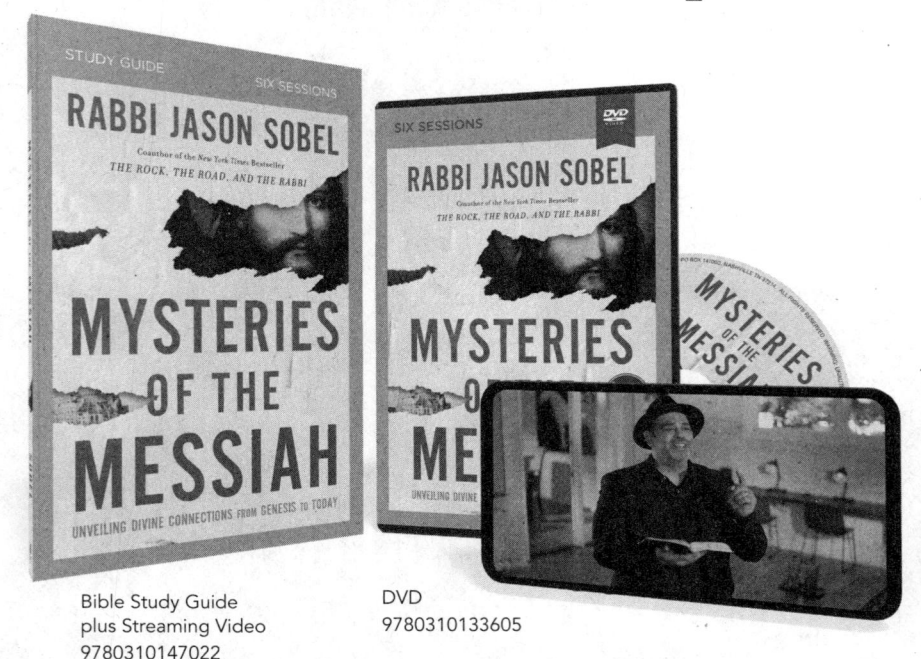

Video Study for Your Church or Small Group

In this six-session study, Kathie Lee Gifford helps you apply the principles in *The Rock, the Road, and the Rabbi* to your life. The study guide includes video notes, group discussion questions, and personal study and reflection materials for in-between sessions.

Study Guide
9780310095019

DVD
9780310095033

Available now at your favorite bookstore,
or streaming video on StudyGateway.com.

HarperChristian
Resources

From the Publisher

GREAT STUDIES

ARE EVEN BETTER WHEN THEY'RE SHARED!

Help others find this study

- Post a review at your favorite online bookseller

- Post a picture on a social media account and share why you enjoyed it

- Send a note to a friend who would also love it—or better yet, go through it with them!

Thanks for helping others grow their faith!